T0193219

PERFECTED
FOR THE
PURPOSE

THE LESSON IS NOT ALWAYS
AND ONLY MINE

ATTELSEA OVERMYER

WestBow
PRESS®
A DIVISION OF THOMAS NELSON
& ZONDERVAN

WestBow Press books may be ordered through booksellers or by contacting:

WestBow Press
A Division of Thomas Nelson & Zondervan
1663 Liberty Drive
Bloomington, IN 47403
www.westbowpress.com
844-714-3454

ISBN: 978-1-6642-9667-1 (sc)
ISBN: 978-1-6642-9668-8 (hc)
ISBN: 978-1-6642-9666-4 (e)

Library of Congress Control Number: 2023906217

Print information available on the last page.

WestBow Press rev. date: 05/10/2023

CONTENTS

CHAPTER 1

INTRODUCTION

**If you see in a province the oppression of the poor and
the violation of justice and righteousness, do not be
amazed at the matter, for the high official is watched
by a higher, there are yet higher ones over them.
Ecclesiastes 5:8**

I am no longer amazed by the messages and signs the Lord has
given me over the last several years, I am honored he has allowed
me to go through the many trials; guiding my steps, humbling me,
strengthening me and making my path clear before me.

**For many are called, but few are chosen.
Matthew 22:14**

This is my story, a true story about requesting, receiving, trials,
sustaining, fulfilling, judgment, grace and vindication. We all
have a specific purpose while here on Earth, it may be to raise a
wonderful family, it may to help the unfortunate, it might be to teach
others, create something that enhances our world or possibly to fight
injustice. These are all what our society would deem appropriate or
Godly purposes; but what if their purpose is to harm, to intimidate,
to extort and embrace illegal yet current socially accepted activity;
to abuse their power? Did God create these souls and along the way

they have been corrupted? Can they change and follow the right path? Who is responsible to identify these unacceptable souls and help them get back on the right track? The answer is we all are. Apathy is not nor should not be an accepted response stating, "that's just the way it is" and "you can't change the system" as taking this attitude is what created the corruption and left unchecked will lead us to further destruction.

Having firsthand experience of the justice system in my state I know of what Einstein spoke. Did he know how dangerous apathy or indifference is to our society? Feeling we are powerless over those that own our system of justice. God has given me great insight into the corruption that exists here in my county and expands daily; experiencing those who you believed to be incorruptible succumbing to the pressure to just let it go. I will be honest I didn't think it was possible. I hope I am wrong, and you will do the right thing. You know who you are.

I believe God lead me through the fire, guiding me every step of the way allowing me eventually to help expose the corruption in our court system especially here where I live and at the very least expose some of the corrupt police officers, attorneys, prosecutors, politicians and judges, they are known and are quite open about how the system works. This widespread corruption has become commonplace, and it is sad but true that few question them. "I know God will provide the exact setting when the time is right as his timing is perfect. I first need to finish this writing which started in 2015 and await next steps." I wrote this last statement in 2015 and it is now 2022 and it is now the right time and the right setting as the corruption has formally been revealed. To non-believers and maybe even professed believers you may question that this is possible, to be led but I assure you we all have this capability you just need to ask and if you hear, be patient and he will guide your steps and make your path straight before you. Your mission is within reach, you will finish your race, as will I.

I have delayed publishing this writing for many years because I don't know if I am ready to share and be once again investigated, and maligned but God is my refuge and fortress and I know he is with me always; and again, I will have no real peace until I finish it. I asked for a reprieve on several occasions and well the answer was always no. Until I focused once again on telling my story he would make it very uncomfortable, having no peace until I would once again work on it as it was and is not for my benefit but written for others to hear, glorifying God and his ultimate protection of us in his justice.

In the Spring of 2016, I wrote that I thought God was giving us one more chance. I didn't know exactly why I felt this or what was to come, but I did confirm in June of 2016 that Trump would win the election. President Trump is flawed as all of us are, but God knows his heart and knew before he was born where he was to serve; God makes no mistakes. This President has the gift of strength that enabled him to persevere through the invasion of his and his family's privacy, the lies, the impeachments, the pandemic and the riots and of course the FBI raid of his home. It is one manufactured crisis after another meant to harm our democracy and take our liberties from each American and this I know without any doubt. There is a purpose when going through trials and there are lessons in it for all of us.

The Devil wants nothing more than to be your friend, disguising his evil quite often through deceptive beings telling you to trust them that their way is the only way. This could be your family, a friend, a trusted advisor, your church, the government or the many forms of media telling you what to think. Do not buy in to everything you may hear and do think first as the wrong decision will only affect our future generations to their detriment; be prudent.

For my safety I have been advised not use the actual names of the many individuals involved. These individuals are very powerful in this state and have ties with even higher authorities in the country. For the record I have no issue with sharing these names once again should the State or Federal authorities request this of me. I believe this should happen, but I am not confident this will occur. My purpose for sharing my experience is based not only on doing what is right, seeking justice, and having some hand in changing the system but if it helps others understand their God given calling and trusting him to bring you through it then I have fulfilled the biggest part of what God has asked of me.

Secondary is the exposure of the current situation in our court system and as well some higher agencies and pray others will come forward after reading this. We can elicit change if we come together, we will fail apart. God is watching, be brave and do the right thing. He will reward you if not in this lifetime, then in the next. I know you possibly have heard that before and maybe you don't want to wait, you want your reward now. My answer to that is if you are on the right path, you will feel rewarded, trust me you will feel it down deep.

In January of 2012 I once again asked God what my purpose was remembering that he told me at the age of five that I indeed had one. Remember that old saying be careful what you ask for? Well, when you're ready God is ready and just know you are either in or you are out there no gray area. You are now on the narrow path walking with Jesus and in your journey, you will learn to speak the truth, make no excuses, follow though, take one thing at a time, listen and ultimately hear what he is telling you. This takes a while, not to learn really but to obey. You know we are told God loves you and will forgive you anything … I do believe this but when you are truly in the walk, he has little patience in reformation at least that is what it feels like. He will use everything and every person to get you there. Creating me new, getting me ready for what I feel is my purpose while I am here on earth was a crazy experience fraught with fear, incredible pain, many questions, fervent prayer, many answers, through many messengers and oh the many confirming signs. He will not give you more than you can handle as he sustains us.

**He who began a good work in you will carry
it on to completion until the day of Christ Jesus.
Philippians 1:6**

As I stated earlier my purpose at least one of them at this time is to help expose some of the existing corruption in the court system in my state. This has been a long journey that is still not over as every time I think this writing is complete, I get yet another validation of corruption not only pertaining to my case but stories of others; delaying the publishing, but God's timing is perfect, isn't it? If you are reading this, then it is your story too as you may live here, and you most likely have children or planning on it and possibly you have grandchildren, and I can't believe you would not want to do everything to secure future generations. My hope in writing this is that others will become more aware and those aware come forward, tell the truth and seek change. The ultimate purpose however is to let others know God exists and has your back and he wants you to not just exist while you are here but make a difference. He will reward you with consistent sustaining and peace that allows you to continue through whatever trials you may have on your path.

**So, whoever knows the right thing to do
and fails to do it, for him it is a sin.
James 4:17**

It may not at first make sense to act on some of the things he wants us to do, especially in my case when acting on his directive had repercussions that have harmed me in this current world, and it mattered not that I was doing the right thing. He does give us our victories, sending us signs letting us know he is here with you and that you are not alone.

I believe God is closest to us as children and it isn't unusual that we hear his voice and as I said I did just that when I was very little. Children are open and positive, inquisitive and not jaded by the world around them; they are open to all the possibilities. Having said that I feel it is so important for children to be listened to and believed as my father believed me. Telling a child that they were probably mistaken in what they heard is the wrong thing to do as children will listen to their parents and then possibly dismiss what they're hearing, what a shame for them. As Christians, do we really believe only the few prophets of the Bible, heard from God? I think not.

I first knew Jesus at the age of five, hearing about him from my parents, especially my Father and in Sunday school but also hearing directly from him. As a child you hear but don't understand but know when you are ready, he will prepare you and get you on your way to fulfilling your purpose he deemed for you before you were born.

I was often told by my mother I was not planned as I was the last of four children but being last does have its benefits; like no one is watching what you're up to or where you are most of the time, but it also meant you got the hand me downs; this was a certainty. In this case on this day this hand me down was a blue Schwinn bike handed down from my sister. My dad wasn't home during the week as he traveled but he made up for it on the weekends and he was ready to help me learn to ride alone. I got on my bike and my dad gave me a push and I was off around the neighborhood.

As I was circling the terrace as I did so many times before I heard a voice saying, "but I wasn't supposed to come back" … and then I heard a very different voice say, "but you have a purpose." That was it. I went to my dad and told him something to this effect as any five-year-old could and he said that was ok, he smiled and said he expected nothing less. He wrote it down and every year he showed it to me and asked if I remembered that day; I did. I don't know at the age of five that I truly comprehended the message, but my father did, and I think he just knew he needed to be my memory and keep that memory safe for me when I was ready. I never understood the 'but I wasn't supposed to come back" message I heard, as the Bible does not believe in reincarnation, but it possibly had to do with my mother having a miscarriage before I was conceived so maybe I was that miscarriage sent again as there are no mistakes.

Before I formed you in the womb I knew you, before you were born, I set you apart; I appointed you as a prophet to the nations. Jeremiah 1:5

CHAPTER 2

THE EARLY YEARS

I grew up in my hometown of Leawood Kansas, attending Sunday school, saying grace before dinner and saying my nightly prayers.

Now I lay me down to sleep, I pray the Lord my soul to keep if I should die before I wake, I pray the Lord my soul to take. God bless Mommy and Daddy, Grandma and Grandpa, my siblings and of course the pets.

I now know going to Church was a social necessity for my mother much like the country club was and it may have been all for show as it is for many who go to church thinking that is enough, but only God knows your heart. My Mother made sure we always had nice clothes and a quarter put in our gloves for the offertory plate. She read a lot, mostly magazines both fashion and home decorating. I am thankful she gave me my sense of style and training in the social graces, but I am also thankful to her for never giving me much encouragement or accolades because to this day I believe it made me a very humble servant, not looking for the limelight but just making sure the things that needed to be done got done. So, in reality this was a gift in disguise, and we need to identify these gifts in our lives and embrace them as they mold you into the person, he wants you to be. Don't resist, it's your path to him.

My Father was a Deacon and a true believer of which I really didn't know the full extent of his devotion to the Lord until many years later and right before his death. He loved me and my mother believed I was his favorite although I know he never would admit that, as he was a good father and loved us all. My mother always said it though and I didn't know why she did, but it would make sense to me later. He called me his Tinkerbelle; you know from Peter Pan; a twinkling light, and I was going to do great things or so he told me. I remember being so happy when he was home which was not that often at least not during the week. He had a big job and did incredibly well for someone with only a high school education, coming from a little town in the Midwest and a family of thirteen children.

He told the story of how his brothers, and he went to enlist after the Japanese had bombed Pearl Harbor. He became a Navy Corpsman serving in the 2ND Marine Division eventually landing on Tarawa, an uninhabitable island in the South Pacific and a historic battle. He was shot an inch away from his heart and recovered in Hawaii at Pearl Harbor. The bullet went right through him as the scars on his chest and on his back proved but it didn't kill him as God had plans for this young man. The bullet didn't kill him, but the navy ship possibly did as he and many others developed a lung condition called mesothelioma although never diagnosed in his early years. I only recently found this out as something kept prompting me to investigate further. Once again, I couldn't shake this feeling and I requested reports from the lung specialist we had taken my father to six months before he died. It was confirmed but he never told us; that was so like him serving valiantly until the very end.

Serving as a corpsman he saw a lot of death, but he also saved many men. He said God had his back, kept him safe and helped him to heal others. After his recovery he stayed in Hawaii working at the Hospital attending to the wounded men and while there he implemented a program that he somehow knew would help those soldiers that had recovered physically but still had not recovered psychologically, something now called Post Traumatic Stress Disorder or PTSD. He started the healing by driving these soldiers around the island stating if God's creation, as beautiful as it was could not calm their souls and heal them then nothing would. I am sure he was right.

God loved my Father and years later proved to him once again with what my Father said was "from the man upstairs himself "a very special gift. Working in Chicago quite often over the years and while walking along Michigan Avenue one day in the Fall of 1970 he was called back by a man passing by him. It seems this man had served with my Father in the Second Marine Division and credits my Father with saving his life that day in the battle of Tarawa. I understood the man's wounds were so severe my dad thought he would never survive the next few minutes let alone the evacuation. Knowing this, he prayed and made the decision to keep him comfortable which they were instructed to do. Many ampoules of morphine were used to quiet his screams and my Father said he thought he killed him that day, not waiting for God to take him. This haunted him for many years as this was not what he was about, he healed he didn't destroy. What are the chances that these two men would pass each other thirty years later let alone recognize each other? I do believe God does give us miraculous gifts and what a gift he gave to these two men meeting a world away as young men and then again on the same street years later; only God could make that happen and give that gift. I know I have seen his miraculous timing and signs and love for his children so very often.

My Fathers brothers did all serve in some capacity during this time in our country's history, but the miraculous thing was they all came home alive. This family was blessed. I didn't know my father's mother as she died shortly before I was born but I remember my grandfather and of course my Aunts and Uncles and I don't ever remember my Dad saying one bad word about any one of them that was not his way or theirs.

After his service in World War II, he considered becoming a physician, but he instead went into the pharmaceutical industry and proceeded to do quite well. In 2005 and a few months before his death I do remember him warning us at one of our many family dinners that the pharmaceutical industry, specifically one that he had worked for was going down the wrong road and what was to come with their great power and influence would be no surprise. How very prophetic his statement was and is a warning for us all. He eventually changed industries working instead with a company interested in animal health and did not retire until he was well into his seventies continuing to consult on a full-time basis. While I was attending college, I typed his letters and visited him at his office, he always had words of wisdom for me and of course a kind word, his usual greeting would be "hey, you're looking good kid!"

He was also a Mason, whom many have heard of, but few understand. Freemasonry is not a religion although they do believe in God; it is a fraternity of like-minded men helping good men to become great men and to help make the world a better place. That was and has remained their promise although some over the years may have distorted their laws leading to much gossip. It was quite fitting that he was part of the Masons, and I don't know how often he went to meetings over the years, but he always wore his ring which he gave to me a month before he died; I guess he must have known. I have it in my possession, just like the truth and foremost my faith.

My parents continued to go to church after we moved to another state, and we continued in the Presbyterian Church where I was proud to attend Sunday school every week and eventually sing in the choir made up of only high school students. All I could think about during my junior high years was singing in this choir and it's as if God was calling me to share my voice and make use of those piano lessons. You see I didn't need braces on my teeth so she reconciled I could have piano lessons instead. That is at least what she told everyone, but I believe she knew when I was very little, I had a passion for music based on tinkering on our neighbor's Steinway every time I came with her when she went to visit her. They would have their coffee in the kitchen, and I would sit and play on the piano but very quietly. I was only to learn from her right before her death that she loved when I played for her. I think I always knew this, but it was nice to hear her say it. I started piano lessons when I was nine years old after asking for years and I don't think she had a choice but to give me these lessons. My teacher enjoyed his many naps during my lessons and would only wake up when I hit a wrong note; I rarely hit wrong notes. He was kind of cranky, but I charmed him as is my nature, this at least was what I've been told. Just recently I sold my parents' house and my piano to a young family. I wanted to take my piano with me but moving a very old baby grand piano was not suggested and I felt very sad until I found out that the little girl who moved into the house was going to take lessons and was very excited. She was nine years old the same age that I was when I started so another sign, and another gift.

Once in the Church choir I found my place. Our choir had at least seventy-five high school kids all singing from their hearts. We recorded albums and visited other churches even in other states, sharing the Good News of the Gospel. I loved my life, and those piano lessons came in handy as I was also one of the accompanists. I was like every other teenager; going to school, working part time and attending Church. I was not perfect as none of us are, but I always knew Jesus was with me guiding my path and keeping me safe. During my junior year of high school, the choir visited a sister church in another state, where we were to perform our latest Christian musical. We stayed at the local Inn and during our stay some of the senior girls of the choir had met a high school baseball team that was in the State Finals. Well kids being kids and not a chaperone in sight, and their mistake taking us to a state that had an age eligibility of eighteen to drink, one thing led to another and a party in one of the rooms ensued. This didn't last very long and was harmless but was a topic of conversation when we got back.

The Pastor called a meeting with the parents and proceeded to call it blasphemy and tell us what bad Christians we were; let the stoning commence. My Father; being the man he was stood up and asked him where the chaperones were when this was taking place and went on by asking when is it a sin to show Christian values by getting to know each other and why didn't the chaperones take the opportunity to show leadership by talking to this special team of young athletes? Dead silence, and a reflective time for all in the room and once again only God could make this happen. Not getting a timely response with his questions he proceeded to quote our Lord, "Ye without sin cast the first stone" and proceeded to walk out with my shocked but quite proud mother following him and myself right behind them. As I turned around to look at my friends there were several other parents getting up and following suit. Victory, thank you God! I know there will be many in the church who will say this is not the Christian way, but I will tell them even Jesus got fed up with the piety and God wants us to stand up and do the right thing.

Even on the day my father died he asked me if I had found my purpose; I said I didn't know. I considered it a gift that I got to know my father better in his last few months of life as. I had a job that I traveled regularly between four states but was stationed in the mid-west and I worked out of my home so I could stop by and see him more often. I do not think this was by chance and it was a gift God gave to me, to spend time and get to know him all over again. He was a wonderful, kind and principled man and I loved him and respected him. I was not prepared for him to die that day as he showed no imminent signs but in early August 2005, I had the feeling he would not be here for very long.

I wanted to have an 85th birthday celebration for him that month but my mother said no but she did however say yes to a dinner for their anniversary in mid-September. I called my sister in California who had not been in to visit for two years and told her of my feeling and that she needed to come in and I also told my other sister who had not seen my father since April of that year due to a quarrel with my mother; I told her she needed to make up with our Mother and consider our Father. We celebrated September 20th, and he died October 20th. I realized what a gift hearing of things to come or others would call "intuition" was once again. We would not have been able to celebrate this man together and enjoy him one last wonderful time before he was gone. Spending time with him was meant to be and knowing I had a specific purpose was just between the three of us; God, my Father and me.

A month after he passed, I found a penny, mind you a bright

shiny penny in a parking lot at the very front of my parked car. Something prompted me to turn around, look up and see it as I don't know I would have otherwise. Well after picking it up and examining it I realized it had the year of my birth printed on it. What are the chances of finding such a thing; old but shiny and new? This was a gift and from this day on and to today when I am going through a tough day God throws me a penny and I put it next to my heart. We are not alone.

"My Mother" chosen by God to be so

Through it all my mother who taught me so much but often showed little affection I can only try to understand why she was the way she was. I don't know if it was from her childhood as I could never seem to get a straight answer. One minute it was of neglect and domestic violence, and another was that she was her parent's savior in their later years. We would visit them each summer and my grandfather was the Justice of the Peace where they lived and I remember him being a loving but a bit distant man. He did possibly have a temper, but he did his best as most Christians strive to do so there is no blame just striving for understanding my Mother. Her Mother was a wonderful woman and her family had been among the first settlers here in the America's and is the reason we are part of The Daughters of the American Revolution (DAR) and something that I am extremely proud of. We should not discount our heritage as something to be ashamed of or apologize for our "white privilege" as many would like us to adopt; but embrace it and demonstrate our patriotism to others coming to this country seeking a safe haven and opportunity called the American Dream. Extend the help but to only those who want to acclimate, to join in and not tear down.

My mother was a fun and interesting person, but she did have her issues and the day before I started high school of which I was so excited for and her knowing this maybe she just wanted to put things in perspective for me; she informed me that I was a mistake.

The story was that she had suffered such severe scar tissue from having my brother, who was a breach birth that her doctor stated that she could have an abortion. This story got brought up over the years, of course never when my father was present, but I do remember one time however it being different; she still told of her incredible difficult delivery with my brother, but this time she stated that through it all she believed having me had actually healed her. I don't believe she even remembered saying this, but God does have his ways and it was a message I needed to hear and just at the right time.

One other memory of our relationship occurred right before my junior year of high school, and I was so looking forward to the new school year. She stated we were going shopping and we were going to go to the beauty salon, and I could "get those bangs you wanted before you go back to school." It was not cutting bangs she had in mind but as I sat in the chair the stylist told me to bend my head forward and she proceeded to cut off my hair that was to my waist to just under my ears. I am assuming they must have been friends and discussed this ahead of time, but I cannot imagine any woman would agree to do this let alone a woman doing it to her own daughter. I was devastated and cried all the way home and when my father saw me, he was outraged with her and told her never to touch me again. Well hair does grow back and even though I did have shorter professional hair over the years I always had double the hair I should have. It was fine, thick and naturally blonde and to this day I have it to my waist. God blessed two-fold so to those of you out there that have suffered loss of any kind, great or something seemingly small and inconsequential as this; just remember God knows all, remembers all, rewards all that love him and restores all that is lost. He refines you through your experiences and makes you ready; there are no mistakes.

Letter to my Mom

I know you loved me in your own way and really the only way you knew how, and I was so glad to have the time we spent before you passed, the Mother I knew that existed deep inside. I forgot how funny you could be. I forgave you years ago for what you put me through as a child and forgave you for the maligning in recent years not knowing what I had gone through and just assuming I was at fault, you were not alone. I will equate it to your dementia and those around you that had your ear and took advantage of your vulnerability. Your attorney, of twenty years knew you had not gone to the doctor in eight years and knew your capacity had changed yet she continued to take your calls listening to your stories and charging you her hourly fee every time you called her. Your son capitalizing on your dementia, taking you to your attorney to change the executor to him after I took care of all of it for sixteen years at yours and Dad's request. The woman at the bank who insinuated herself in your life, taking your calls to chat and to gossip in order to maintain your account balances at the bank. I was thankful you allowed a doctor that I knew from church to come to your house to talk to you but it was a shame that your son came home and proceeded to order him to leave the house. I know you would have been happier and more peaceful under a doctors' care, and he was such a good man. Through all however, God strengthens us who believe, and I pray he heals our family so we can move forward together as we once were as children. After your oldest daughter and my sister died, I felt your pain as it was not an easy time for any of us, but I do believe she came to you after her death appearing to you as a child. Some would say you were hallucinating, which was entirely possible based on your condition, but I did feel it was a comfort to you that only God could provide. You didn't know this but every time you called 911 telling the police your little girl was missing, they would contact me, and I would call you and hopefully make you less frightened telling you she just went home for the night, and she would be back to see tomorrow.

Before I had filled out what was called a premise report asking the police to contact me in the event of your calling 911 a very kind officer that I knew from the church had already been to your house to hear your concerns about the little girl. I was speaking to him one day while I was on security duty at the church and quite by chance, and we know nothing is by chance he asked me where I lived, and I told him about you and that you lived down the street in the next town over and he said, "you mean Martha"? I laughed and realized you had already left a lasting impression on the local police and this one specifically. He said he had spoken to you a couple of times and although he realized you were hallucinating, he said you were very articulate and quite convincing which we both knew that to be true, but that was your way which made it hard for people to believe me that you had dementia.

I believed for years you were inhabited by less than honorable forces as I believe many of the elderly may experience based on their diminished capacity. It is just a theory I have and telling my friends of this they all laughed at the suggestion but did not discount it. Once they heard that you had used a walker since you broke your hip in 2007 but that you no longer even used a cane to get around and that you were now faster than greased lighting, they did believe me especially my two friends that were nurses. In January of 2017, a few months before your death I remember you being so angry at me for calling the cable company to fix a failed connection and that this man was in your house. You proceeded to sit on the chair in the foyer and I on the steps leading to the dining room when I asked you who I was speaking to as I wanted to identify who was causing you such distress; without waiting for an answer, I proceeded to tell Satan that he no longer had any power here and to get behind me. You bowed your head and after over a minute of silence you lifted your head and replied to my question; 'I'm your mother who do you think I am?" I believed in my heart whatever force that held you had released you at that minute. I know God granted me this gift to discern, identify and banish evil as this ability is given to all that follow him although

I don't know if many believe this as it is not widely preached in our churches these days.

I know God spoke to you those last few days of your life and maybe many others that have passed on. I especially thought so after seeing your hands reaching to the sky while lying in your hospital bed … your lips moving, and your eyes closed. I wondered who you were speaking to as it was very clear to me you were having a conversation with someone. I waited until you woke to ask you who you were talking to, and you proceeded to tell me very indignant that "your father, he blames me for all the trouble with you kids and said I should just stop it and get up here!" I couldn't help but laugh out loud and you were not happy with me, but I believe you did take the connection to heart and just maybe you had heard from others that had passed on as well. I was very lucky to have spent time with you before you left us, and I will be forever grateful one of the last things you said to me was that you were so proud of me and when I asked why you were proud of me you said, "you know." The amazing thing is I never told you the details about what I went through, so I know God works in miraculous ways; he gave us both a gift that day, me with my prayer of vindication and you with forgiveness and eternal life with him.

We are all mothers to someone

I am not a mother and as much as I dreamed of having children it was not to be as I suffered ovarian failure in my thirties. My niece is my kid as I always have told her and who I still hug and give kisses to every time I see her just as I did when she was a baby. I do believe she was supposed to be mine as I have told her, and we do have a special relationship since she was born while I was still in my teens. I know my sister and her husband loved her so much, did a great job and provided well for her. I have always been there for her and will always be there to love her and guide her when she lets me especially as her mother un-expectantly passed away in 2016. To lose a mother at a relatively young age is shocking and I don't know everything she feels but she seems to have accepted it. She got married that next year and became a mother the very next year delivering a very special baby boy on a special date remembered that being September 11th and a beautiful little girl just two years later. I know my sister watches over her and is with my dad and mom and the many animals she loved that have passed on. She is missed and there isn't a day I don't think of her, and she knows I am there for her daughter. I was and will continue to be her Auntie, her mentor when she lets me, and her confidant, someone in this world who would never betray her and know she will always come first. God brought her into this world and allowed me to be her biggest fan.

She was baptized as a baby but is not a follower of the Lord but believes in a higher power. I have challenged her that can't that higher power be Jesus and you just haven't asked him his name? I challenge all people who feel something is there alongside them but just not sure what it is. My advice, ask him for a sign and then you will know. I have also suggested it is her responsibility to understand Christianity and really all religions to truly know and understand her students even though religion is not tolerated in our schools today, but she has promised me she will consider this. I am very proud of her as she knew her calling early on. I once heard that you start with a job you then have your career and finish with your vocation. She skipped the first two and went right to vocation as she is a teacher in the city, teaching special education to high school students in a minority area of the city. When my mother asked her a few years back why she didn't teach in the suburbs she stated that she would not leave the city's public schools because she is needed there. I agree, she is a gift to the kids, and she makes a difference and will continue to do so. God knows this city's public schools can use honorable teachers, whether their union leaders are or are not.

CHAPTER 3

"PERFECTED FOR THE PURPOSE"

We all have a purpose and God does not forget and he makes sure you fulfill your purpose if you believe and ask and continue to be led. Don't let others, even your church pastor tells you that having a special purpose or having a unique gift isn't in the cards for everyone, that your good works are dead works, and you are only saved by grace alone. This type of talk even though in the chapter of Hebrews can be misinterpreted and may cause many to feel they need not do anything even if they know they have heard from God and know their calling. Again, open yourself, listen and ultimately hear what he is saying to you then move forward. Religion will not do it for you, and people in church will not do it for you, and your pastor will not do it for you. This is a personal relationship and God is the only one that is there every minute of your journey. Ask to hear his direction and he will allow you an open portal. God gives you messengers, God gives you helpers, but it is ultimately God that refines you for your purpose and sustains you, nothing else. You become just that; perfected for your purpose.

Early in 2011 I met a very nice man, he was a Christian, divorced, an engineer and a former Navy Seal, perfect! He was everything I thought I wanted. He was respectful, kind, smart, affectionate and worldly. We enjoyed each other's company having many deep conversations often of God and sometimes about his former profession. I felt he had many unresolved issues about his days in the military, but I didn't press him on it. We spoke about our previous relationships, and he didn't understand why his previous marriage didn't work out. I to this day do not have any ill will towards my past relationships, as I consider them good men but just not the right man for me. He spoke about his ex-wife quite often and I did tell him that maybe he should try to reconcile. He said maybe it was his fault, but it probably wouldn't happen as she had moved on and was with someone else now. We did not continue in our relationship as he was not ready, and I do feel it was not the right time for me. Before we broke up however, he did tell me he thought I had healed him. At the time I thought how odd that he would say this but remembering my mother also told me this helped me understand. God brings the people you need into your life for many purposes, and we are vessels; we are the messengers he calls upon to minister to those in need whether physically or it may be for just a brief time delivering his message to them. If you believe that God has already planned your life, then this all makes sense, doesn't it? Let me continue.

The Ask

After many successful years in Business, I had recently been downsized, something I had never experienced, so during this interim I was consulting on my own and waiting for that next big corporate job. When I left jobs, I was always recruited so this was a little different and I didn't quite know how to feel about it. I was unjustly let go as it came to my attention that only employees with family responsibilities were kept and being single made you expendable. This happened to many in this organization and there were many lawsuits filed but few were successful as this organization was very connected. On December 31, 2012, I asked God what my purpose was and with that I was thrown into the deep end of everything I had no experience in. I didn't really understand all the signs until much later but realized God was preparing me and you live life going forward but you understand it backwards; it came quite fast and furious.

That same week, at the exact same place but within days of each other; I met two devout Christian women. I thought this was coincidental, but nothing happens by chance. I asked God to reveal my purpose and he started preparing me by bringing these two women into my life that were much older than I was and well wiser. They were to become my mentors; my sisters in Christ named Betty Phyllis and Barbara Jenn. My meeting with Betty was a "divine appointment" as she called it as that day, she decided to take this God mandated appointment of giving her testimony to me instead of her scheduled appointment with her Doctor; he could wait; talking to me about God could not. Betty told me of the church she attended which was just down the street from where I lived and invited me to attend but first, I had to hear her testimony right then and there. She was a true believer and had suffered through continued physical ailments. At the age of 41 she suffered a heart attack and literally died on the table but was revived and survived and later that year she was diagnosed with cancer. She was in her seventies and had survived all those years by faith and knowing God had her here for a reason and she was known as a miracle in the medical community. She passed away a few years ago and she will be missed by many. What can I say about her, she knew her Bible and could talk your ear off when she was not taking care of her husband and her grandkids and of course when reading the Bible. She listened to your concerns and would remedy them for you by quoting scripture and life's lessons and her experience in those lessons.

As I stated I met Betty the same week I met Barbara; what are the chances? It became apparent to me that they were the reinforcements that were to be by my side as I met them before my ordeal and trial began. Barbara was also seventy years old and had just lost her husband to a sudden heart attack the month before I met her. I feel God brought us together to help each other on our next journey and season of our lives since she lost her husband and I had asked for God to reveal his purpose for me. She also invited me to a church service that met on Saturday nights. She was a retired Emergency Room Nurse and again was a devout Christian that knew her bible inside and out. She had recently left her church of 40 years listening to God as she prayed for her new path. Although I knew the Bible, I became her student and she was my mentor, but she was always opened to hear my opinion and in this I believe we helped each other in many areas.

I went to this church on Saturday nights with her and then went to the church that Betty went to on Sunday mornings. At this church I was amazed by a specific Pastor's gift of teaching. It seemed God was talking directly to me through this man, and I am to this day still listening. What is also interesting about this church is that a neighbor of mine years earlier had invited me to this church as well so again it was meant to be. On Sunday's I would come into the Sanctuary and sit by myself, and I never really felt alone as God was with me and I was use to traveling across the country on business and being alone so nothing really ever scared me or deterred me. I do hope that all churches would be more inviting to those attending alone and I would tell the leadership not to put them in a box, assuming you know who they are for the judgment could be and is often wrong. Talk to them and get to know them, don't assume and judge as you don't know what they have gone through or do you know their story. Although judgment was easily seen and felt and was experienced on a regular basis attending this church I still on Sunday's would get up, get ready and while driving to the church I would ask Jesus to give me a sign that he still wanted me to continue attending. I know it seems inappropriate, but he gave me a front row parking spot every Sunday regardless of the time I got there, and this still happens and well, he does have a sense of humor and after all I did ask him for a sign. It continues to this day, ten years later and when he fails to deliver this front row parking spot, I will know its time to move on but today I am still there.

Later that year Barbara decided to start going to this church with me on Sundays. She said she was through with this other church that she was a member of for over forty years which was kind of funny to hear but when Barbara decides, she is all in or all out no gray area for her. She senses the answer from him and moves forward, no regrets, she has learned some lessons as she will admit but she still moves forward. I liked her style and continue to stay in contact although she has moved away. They were to be with me educating me in his ways and answering my many questions. They were there for me but neither knew fully what happened to me.

I did try to tell my story to the Pastors in my church but more than once I was shut down which I find troubling at the very least them being men of God, but this did serve a purpose. You realize God wants you to depend on him entirely, those in the world sometimes distract from this so it becomes necessary. Yes, you would think they would have your best interest at heart, but I don't blame them as they have their own walk with God. I kept what happened to me from all; never telling my story except to one man and someone God led me to. There are no coincidences as he is a retired agent who on a regular basis sought justice. I hope as he reads this, he knows how grateful I was as he was someone who I could talk to and share my many inexplicable encounters with corruption. He knows who he is and as I have told him many times; God has more for you to do.

CHAPTER 4

"THE LESSON IS NOT ALWAYS AND ONLY YOURS"

The lesson is often someone else's and you are only the messenger and I continue referring to this when I feel abandoned in the world because God does use all of us to teach others, through circumstances and to all including those that should know better and even when they may never acknowledge that the lesson is theirs. Do not ever discount what your friends, family or even a perfect stranger tells you, just be open, listen and hear and take the time to reflect. God communicates regularly and over the years many of my friends will tell me something only to immediately say they had no idea why they said it, but they just felt they had to. There are many answers to your prayers and many directions he will give you. Heed them is my advice because delaying well is just that a delay although I do believe through every lack of discipline we are further refined and better prepared. The lesson is often hard but often for a good reason. Over the years I have been blessed with having great insight and could anticipate upcoming events and I have developed a better understanding of these and do not dismiss them as lightly as I did in the past. I have had insights into two major disasters and more recently the power outages targeting our electric grids. I have regrets thinking maybe I could have done something to prevent them but sadly it was only a feeling then and two such major and tragic U.S events happened within a few years of each other and then I only had vague thoughts in relationship to their happening and since then I have asked God to expand this gift allowing me better clarity which he has delivered to me but there are too many to tell.

For years I had traveled via air across the country for business and never once felt any concern for my safety. A few months before that fateful day in September 2001, I couldn't shake this feeling of dread concerning air travel and well, aircraft in general. I told my women's business group of my concerns about flying and they just laughed knowing how much I traveled over the years. I was so sure and not shaking the feeling and while planning a family trip in the summer of 2001 I decided to ensure my sister and niece's safety and put them on a separate flight from me. We traveled on August 11th and my plane was grounded for four hours before we took off. A month later I would understand my feeling, yes, I sensed something but not enough to prevent it. I was devastated as we all were on that day as I watched the second plane crash into the towers, but I also could not shake a feeling that many in the then current administration knew about it, dismissed it and possibly could have prevented it. It got us into a war and well a handful of good ole boys made a substantial gain at our expense. All those that knew something and said nothing or those that participated will have to live with it and they will be judged.

The next time I had such a feeling was when I was flying out of New Orleans after attending a conference. I always secured an aisle seat but this time I had a window seat with a colleague sitting next to me. Looking out over this city I was overcome with such a feeling of dread that continued for weeks after. I wish I could have told someone as I couldn't have anticipated the catastrophe of Katrina would soon follow. I continue to sense certain things, ask for clarity and hope I can use this gift for good. I know I am at least to shed some light on the blatant corruption in the court system. I can't imagine God giving me so many trials, clear signs and so many factual examples of corruption over the last few years if it was not his intention to use me to expose at least what I know and maybe bring others forward; sharing their stories and initiate change.

When you ask for your purpose God will grant you your wish and use you for his purpose; the purpose he had all along for you. After years of doing the right thing, being a good daughter, excelling in business, and having a stellar reputation it all drastically changed for me. Now I don't blame God for giving me this specific purpose, but I was certainly not ready for the timing of it all and the very dark place it sent me. I asked for my purpose in January 2012, met my two Christian mentors that month, attended this new church in February and experienced the dark side in March, all in less than sixty days. There are no coincidences just paths meant to be followed.

> **So, the tested genuineness of your faith- more
> precious than gold that perishes though it is tested
> by fire- may be found to result in praise and glory
> and honor at the revelation of Jesus Christ.
> Isaiah 41:10**

Not doing anything illegal but being so violently exposed to our current system of justice I can only feel I am where I'm supposed to be as he continues to guide my steps, giving me the opportunity to share my story for his glory; granting me vindication in this world and passing judgment on those that should be held to a higher standard; those that have taken an oath to uphold the law and not use the law for their own monetary, political or egotistical gain. These officials more than likely have been given every benefit in their lives that many of the poor and under privileged have not. To those who have been blessed and give back you are to be thanked; to those given much and continue to take well you will be judged if not in this lifetime, then in the next I assure you. I believe God has passed judgment on these corrupt souls that I speak of based on information I have heard and can confirm, coincidence many would say, but there are no coincidences only God's truth.

**No one enters suit justly; no one goes to law honestly;
they rely on empty pleas, they speak lies, they
conceive mischief and give birth to iniquity.
Isaiah 59:4**

He created the **person for the purpose,** and it is just that simple for me to explain as I had a strong sense of right and wrong and had never experienced an injustice in my profession or at the hands of law enforcement, but this was all going to change. It is interesting that this happened now almost ten years ago and so much of what happened to me has come to light in our country, specifically the mistreatment of women, and the continued corruption of our court system and the more recent; although not new, exposure of corruption in our federal agencies. I have delayed finishing my story, coming up with every excuse not to finish it but I cannot get away from it as every time I think writing this was just cathartic and a way to get over it, I get yet another unsolicited situation presented to me confirming the injustice. I am here finishing this today as I do not intend to disappoint him.

The year started out hopeful, attending a new church and meeting my two new mentors while February 2012 also brought a welcomed job interview at one of the largest Healthcare Systems in the country. The CEO of a previous Hospital Foundation that I had worked for was now heading up the Foundation and asked me to interview for the Senior Director. I was ready to leave and looked forward to a new state and a new job but when I told Betty Phyllis of my job opportunity, she gave me one of many prophetic statements to come. She said, 'I believe you may need to take care of your mother." Did she jinx it? No, I just think God had other plans for me and she was the messenger even if I didn't know it and she didn't know it at the time. I was very excited about the new job opportunity, but God had other plans for me and on a day in March 2012 my life would change forever. When you are doing something in the flesh when God is talking to your spirit, he will get your attention. I do believe God allowed Lucifer himself to test me and I got thrown into the fire just like Job. Now I am not comparing myself to Job but to the testing and refining God allows so that he can get you prepared for the reason you are here on Earth, when you finally get it, that you are on the narrow path, straying does not appeal to you. That however does not mean that God does not want you in the world, he clearly does and uses us to help others through their own trials. He hates injustice and he put that on my heart years ago. No one knows what one is capable of until they go through it. I know he has been with me, refining me but sustaining me. He will not fail me I know this.

When you pass through the waters, I will be with you; and through the rivers, they shall not overwhelm you; when you walk through a fire you shall not be burned, and the flame shall not consume you.
Isaiah 43:2

CHAPTER 5

THE DAY IT ALL CHANGED

When you have the spiritual gift of what some call insight never and I mean never second guess it. God has given this gift to me and any time I have gone against it I have regretted it. You may know what I am talking about so learn from me, always pray and wait and if the feeling still lingers then stay still, don't move until you hear. I have learned over the years that God's voice does still me, and he leads me and remember evil entices you and ultimately condemns if you succumb. Having your God directed path clear before you, you become a major threat to the dark side. Be in the spirit and you will be safe but still know you may go through the fire when you are chosen, and you choose to accept.

The entire week I had such a sense of dread concerning an upcoming event and Fundraiser on that Saturday. It was a wonderful and unseasonably warm day and was also St. Patrick's Day. I kept feeling I shouldn't go but went against my gift and went anyways thinking I would only stay for a while, and everything would be fine. I also had my little Yorkshire terrier at home not feeling well so God gave me every out, but I went against my feeling and went anyways; I would go just for a while. Well, it proved to be very dangerous and what happened that day change my life. It has been ten years and I have learned so much about my faith and God and his plans for me but as well what happened that day has ruined my professional reputation, my family relationships and my position and my reputation in the church I still attend. Many have snapped to judgment, not seeking the facts first, allowing gossip to overcome what is right and just. The outcome and lessons for many will be presented to those in God's time as the lesson is theirs. Through all this I am eternally grateful for the experience and would not change what I have now in the spirit than the enticements of this world; after all we are but a mist, here for only a short time. We need to be of use to him and help make this a better world and not just wait for the next world as many Christians give as a reason for not getting involved. I know I am sustained, and I also know I will be rewarded if not in this world, then in the next but today I am here.

In him we have obtained an inheritance, having been predestined according to his purpose of him who works all things according to the counsel of his will.
Ephesians 1:11

I left in the late morning that Saturday as I was to meet my friend at her house and leave my car as she was picking up a friend as we headed downtown. We decided to park at the medical office building where she worked and take a cab to the fundraiser which was taking place at a major hotel where we decided to have lunch in the bar afterwards. We were surprised to see many of our state police officers partying in the place and since they were in uniform it was not inconspicuous. Some were pretty loud and pretty lewd towards many women in the bar although from what I saw most of the women were willing and active participants. It was after all a major Irish holiday and these officers were in town for the parade that morning and they wanted to party. Not ever being downtown on this yearly event I really didn't know what to expect but I guess I should have in this city. After about an hour of watching this the commanding officer came up to us and apologized for their behavior and then proceeded to ask us if he could buy us drinks. I guess he had other motives other than being responsible for his men, this did not surprise me, and we did not accept his offer and quickly got the check and made our way down the street to the restaurant where my friend's niece was in a presentation of Irish dancing. This was fun being at a true Irish function as they take this tradition of dancing very seriously. Her family was nice, and the dancing was fun to watch but I was ready to head home so we headed back to pick up her car but on the way my friends decided to continue to another restaurant. I declined and told them I would take a cab back to her house which was not that far. This was around five o'clock and it was getting dark as daylight savings time hadn't started yet. I flagged a cab as I had done so many times in this city and around the country, but never could I have anticipated what I was about to encounter.

Getting into that cab proved to be a very dangerous situation but again it was the start of something important. I do believe this cab driver had ideas other than just taking me to my destination. He stated he didn't know how to get to her address, nor did he have GPS and with this I told him I would find another cab, but he said he would agree to a flat fee if I could instruct him on how to get to my destination. This was not uncommon for cabs to make deals such as this, so it did not bother me, and he turned off the meter as a gesture but he did turn it back on at some point. Something still warned me I should have gotten out of the cab, but I felt rushed and remember evil rushes you. He had little patience when dealing with customers or at least with me and I don't believe he drove this cab for very long and I don't believe he was here in this country legally.

I told him to take the Tri state and get off at a major cross street a few miles from her house which was in a very nice community, and I would direct him from there. This was not to be and after getting off the Tri State he proceeded to pull into a pitch-black parking lot where a certain restaurant resided. He parked behind three large trees and did not answer me when I asked him to take me to the gas station across the street. At this point I didn't want him to take me to her house now as I didn't want to be alone with him and to be honest, never experiencing this from a cab driver in my many travels

I was a little afraid of him, and I felt at least I could call another cab from the gas station, and I didn't want to be in his car any longer that is all that I knew.

He said he wasn't going any further and that I owed him sixty-three dollars, he had left the meter on which I did not see because we had a glass window between us, and the meter was down under the dash. I said we agreed on forty and I gave the cash to him through the window, and he took it, and I once again asked him to take me across the street to the Shell station. He refused once again and this time I told him to take me across the street and I would instead give him my credit card and he could charge me the amount on the meter instead of the cash as I now wanted a receipt from him. I didn't know then what his motives were, and I don't to this day; I only knew I needed to get away from him and out of his cab. He refused and at this point he was now yelling at me in another language, and I was honestly scared of him, and he proceeded to lock the doors from his front seat. I informed him I was calling the police if he did not unlock the doors and take me across the street and as I started looking in my purse for my phone to call 911, he tried to reach through the window to stop me. Sufficiently panicked, I hit the button for the windows and down they came, and I went out the window straddling the glass, leaving my phone and purse in the cab. I really don't know what gave me the strength to do this except immense fear and sheer adrenalin just knowing I needed to get away from him out of this dark place and into the light.

Thank the Lord, thank the angels he had protecting me, but it was not without consequences as my right leg was severely damaged and I could barely walk let alone run but God was with me, and I made it to the gas station across a busy four lane local highway. Once inside I told the girl behind the counter to call the police and she did as I heard her talking to them, but the call and her testimony never appeared in the report. The police came within minutes and one of the three officers came up to me handcuffing my hands behind my back while standing in front of me and whispered in my ear to say nothing. I did what he said as I was scared and at this point, I had no reason not to trust him. I can't say at the time I knew any policemen personally and never had any reason to fear them as I only knew that they were here to serve and protect and to this day I don't know why this happened. They never questioned the girl at the gas station even though she told them right in front of me that I asked her to call them. They arrested me and drove me to their station, and I found out later that the cab driver had called his company telling them I had not paid him. I can only assume the company contacted someone in this department's higher ups in this police station and I believe the cab company had a lot to do with the charges and the subsequent outcome in this case. Mind you I had been all over the country taking cabs for years without an incident or even distrusting a cab driver. I know there are other cultures that do not respect women and maybe threatening, intimidating and locking someone in their cab is legal in their country but here it is called **Unlawful Restraint**, which is a felony.

I am sure this man was not here legally and even if he was arrested as he should have been this is a sanctuary city, aiding them even when they are clearly guilty. I was the victim but since they are immigrants, legal or illegal they are given every benefit to insure they are treated fairly. I didn't get that benefit even though I was the clear victim and a US citizen, never getting a ticket let alone arrested. In this case I believe the cab company intervened and some agreement was reached with the arresting officer, not considering what was legal but more likely lucrative. To reiterate, the police who arrested me knew that the cab driver parked across the street in a dark secluded area and not at my destination, they knew he picked me up at the medical building rather than the train station where he said he picked me up, they knew he had changed the amount due and that he had locked me in the car, and they knew I told him I was calling the police. Now mind you they knew all this through **his written statement** which I have in my possession. You may ask how this can happen, but I don't think it is isolated, the abuse of power exists and using that power over women is done more often than we hear. They knew all this information but still decided to charge me with a misdemeanor instead of charging him with Unlawful Restraint which is a class one felony with a jail sentence up to three years and a twenty-five thousand dollar fine. Charging me was the first injustice but the court moving forward on it compounded their responsibility in this matter by proceeding with a case against me and that is called Malicious Prosecution. My attorney should have done the right thing and immediately had the case thrown out instead he went through the motions, covering and collecting.

In light of today's violence and media scrutiny many officers no longer get involved when observing a crime or feeling something looks suspicious, they look the other way and I have been told this by more than one officer I personally know that works in a high crime area. They did however tell me they do have to respond to 911 calls and make an arrest no matter what the circumstances are. The officers have done their job and now the attorney's and the state get involved and the process starts; guilty or not someone pays, and it is not just in cash. The effects of being violated and unjustly accused can have lingering effects especially trusting those that are here to protect you.

Once at the station they instructed me to sit on a bench and within minutes there were many male officers walking by me smiling; one officer saying, "well we got a good one tonight." You could tell they were enjoying themselves, but this eventually ended after a while, and they put me in a locked room even though I was sitting quietly not saying a word. They then brought me before another officer and told me they were charging me with Theft of Services and Battery as it seemed he complained I hit him which was not even possible as we were separated by a glass partition between the front and back seat as in many cabs. I explained this to the officer, but he never listened to me. They proceeded to take cash from my purse and stated they would use it for bail which was over one hundred fifty dollars. When I asked the officer why I would not pay a cab driver when I had all this cash and to this he replied for me to be quiet. He never inquired how I was feeling and never attended to my medical needs; this was such a clear violation of my rights, but it isn't isolated as there have been many victims over the years at the hands of corrupt police officers and it came to my attention a few years later that this police department had a relationship with a cab company; the exact company that was involved in my case. Some feel they are untouchable and there are no consequences, but things do change, and my feeling is today it may not have happened to me as this injustice happened over ten years ago when the body cameras were not mandatory. I do want to say I know several officers now through my service in my church and they are honorable men and women, so I am not accusing the police in general of this type of behavior.

The Police released me and called a cab for me as I didn't want any of my family or friends to have to drive an hour to pick me up. I remember the kind policeman who escorted me out asking me how I could get into a cab now after going through what I just went through. I told him I had taken cabs across the country for the last ten years and I never felt unsafe, and I know he believed me as he helped me into the cab and told me how sorry he was that this happened. Not sorry enough to question his superiors however but I have found out from other officers I consider friends that this is not uncommon as they risk losing their jobs. This code of silence they follow impedes justice and how sad for the righteous officers just wanting to do the right thing; this has to change, and I believe it is changing based on the more recent cases now in the media. The code is not as honorable as they want the brotherhood to be perceived so support your local law enforcement as they are here to serve and protect but also expose the bad as in any other business or government agency. I believe the many recent stories of Police corruption in this state at least have become more prevalent because God is exposing it. I am yet another story, of which there are many even though different; I am not a minority, I am not uneducated, I am not an alcoholic or drug abuser and I am not a gang member or an unfortunate youth that has lost hope. I am a highly educated professional woman that has never been in trouble with the law, and I was an easy target that night and easy to manipulate with the police bending the law to their benefit and most likely the benefit of the cab company.

I do believe the police often pull over and arrest women as it is safer for them and well maybe more interesting as well at least for the male officers. Also, pulling over a white person in a nice car is often perceived as safer but also it is likely more profitable down the road. This is called profiling and it is done and recently I asked an officer that I know if he only pulls over expensive cars as I had seen him three times over a few months pulling over the top-of-the-line vehicles from which he smiled and he said don't be ridiculous. I do want to say I know several officers that are honorable, and they are here to protect and serve but to assume that there are no officers adding to their income through these random often profiled arrests is comical. I personally know a retired officer that is a LinkedIn connection with me who is also a connection to one of the most notorious former prosecutors and an "on the take" attorneys in this area. I would have thought they would be smarter to not advertise their relationship but then again most do not care as they feel they are untouchable. Also remember even the most honorable officer will be targeted by attorney's, prosecutors and even Judges to change a ticket or remember it differently in court under oath. These officers that partake are known and the rest all know this to be true, yet they keep silent.

CHAPTER 6

THE ATTORNEYS

Finding myself in this situation and not knowing any attorney except my family attorney I decided to respond to the direct mail piece I received at my home shortly after the incident. This type of attorney is an extortionist, and they love the easy cases, and they know the addresses that can afford them, secure them a not guilty verdict and some substantial cash and knowing that I was the victim only added to the prize. Bruce Wayne became my first attorney after speaking briefly to his partner on the phone as he stated he didn't handle these cases, but Bruce did, but he also seemed to know what I had gone through before I even started explaining. It didn't occur to me at that time how they knew the details of my case, but it makes sense now knowing what I know and, I believe Bruce Wayne was already being considered for a position with the state so he couldn't be party to soliciting me. I have stated nothing is by chance and I now believe his selection was key to God's plan. I met him at an office that I'm sure he rented and shared with other attorneys as many do. This was not his office that was apparent as it wasn't anyone's office, illusion and smoke and mirrors, intimidation and fear and never experiencing this, how does one know how to hire an attorney; I do now.

The purpose of the first meeting is to insight fear in you by telling you what can happen to you if you are convicted; they then record you as you're telling your side of the story and then they tell you their fees, as this is of the utmost importance, getting the payment. He told me his fee was five hundred dollars to represent me and another five hundred dollars in case we need to go to trial, oh and by the way he needed the entire amount up front. Now you must ask yourself why he would even mention going to trial and equate the two if he didn't already know it would be dismissed. I was so naive and paid him up front, we never went to trial, yet he never reimbursed me the five hundred dollars as he never returned my calls or emails; surprising then but not so surprising now. When hearing my story, he acted like he didn't believe me, again a form of intimidation but he knew I was not guilty as the cab drivers statement confirmed and clearly identified me as a victim not the perpetrator, but this information was not shared with me until after my court date and dismissal. This was a win for him. If it can happen to a professional educated woman than what is happening to those not as fortunate. My thought is that it happens all the time and it's easier to pay and move on than to call them out on it and I guess at the time I was no different, I just wanted it to be over. I just wanted to move on but unfortunately the city's daily paper had other ideas and put my name all over the internet. The story read as this:

Name, age, address was arrested and charged with battery and theft of services after an incident at time and date. A cab driver reportedly picked her up in the city and once they got to her destination, she became verbally abusive, refused to pay and allegedly she slapped the driver in the face, climbed out of a partially open rear window and went to the gas station across the street at (address) where officers located her. She was released on I-bond.

Now of course nothing was mentioned of the cab driver stopping before my destination and parking in a dark secluded lot or that he locked me in his cab. Well, you can imagine how devastating this was for me. Not only was I a victim at the hands of the Police and our court system but now victimized in the press as well. The sad fact is the press is well within their rights and it is not illegal for them to print these stories as it is deemed for the protection of society and their need to know but this clearly is a violation of our rights. Why should anyone arrested be made public when there is every chance, they are not guilty and the victim? I can understand why people just keep it quiet and want it to go away which is what I did but God as you will see if you keep reading kept giving me reason after reason to expose this system and my case is just one example and of course and unfortunately many go unreported.

During the weeks I waited on a court date I had requested my police file via email from my attorney, but I did not receive it until after the dismissal. I know he had it all along even before our first and only meeting but he did not share it with me until after the case was dismissed and then he sent me a copy. This is when I found out that the cab drivers written statement confirmed what happened to me, so many lies and such injustice and even a payout to exonerate a victim. Attorney's feed on this as it makes them money, the courts feed on it as it makes the state money, the prosecutor if corrupt may make some extra cash, the police make their quota and often some extra cash and well the Judge can stop all this but then again, I have found their hands may be tied as well by higher authorities at least in this county. They succumb to the pressure in keeping their job, but it still is illegal. Monitoring the individual Judge's and tracking their decisions is a key component to recovering our justice system.

I hope my story helps and fuels the fire with all the cases now in the news about judicial overreach here and even at the federal level. Being a Judge or prosecutor is not a license to make deals, it is to serve the community by judging fairly, sentencing within guidelines to those guilty and listening to those not guilty. This is the only way to change the system, through the judges and everyone knows it. Sadly, it may never happen as so many embrace the current system as it works for them. Judges who are not willing to compromise, well they probably won't be in position very long. There is a recent case where a newly elected judge just resigned after not wanting to follow the direction of his superiors. More information on this is not available on the internet as this type of press is not good for the judicial business.

In my individual case they were protecting the Police and the cab company and driver, as my attorney said to me "the case is getting dismissed that's what you want right?" He said you know we could risk the case not getting dismissed going before the judge and he could find you guilty; such manipulation and gas lighting, making one to doubt is not uncommon. Remember I did not have the cab drivers written statement at that time, but they did, if I had things would have been different. I should have been smarter, and I was recently told by two different attorneys that are members of my church that I didn't seem the type to be a victim and that maybe I was just setting these men up. Again, trying to divert attention from the legal system and intimidate me but they also told me they believed me, and, in that case, I should have done something about it a long time ago. My response to them was after such apparent corruption and abuse in the court system you become your own advocate and you fight injustice; it makes you a different person. I had no reason to not trust my attorney, after all they are there for you right and you have paid them? If you have any doubts get a second opinion preferably from an attorney that has never been a States Attorney, after all this is where they learn their way around the courts, making connections with the courthouse personnel all the way to the Judges. Yes, I said it! My attorney made money; the court made money; the prosecutor made money not only from me but no doubt from the cab company as well and the Police got off the hook for their actions and deception.

I was instructed by my attorney to be at the courthouse at a certain time but always one to be early I happened upon my attorney speaking to a man in the lobby. I waited until their conversation was over and as the man walked away, I then approached him with him immediately stating that the cab driver had approached him wanting him to represent him and that he told him that was not possible since he was representing me. I didn't believe him and what I believe is he knew I saw them conversing and he told me this to get himself off the hook, but I do also believe Bruce Wayne was representing both of us; myself and the cab company. Also, the man that showed up in court that day was not the same man that drove the cab that night as the man appearing in court was much shorter and spoke better English and when I relayed this to Mr. Wayne, he dismissed me once again telling me I must be mistaken. I don't think the original driver was in this country legally as many are not and only God knows where he is now. Going through this was not easy but I do know he sustained me and at the time I didn't know why this happened, but it was the start of the many instances of corruption uncovered.

The Senior Pastor of my church in one of his sermons stated that having a clear conscience means doing what God has instructed you to do and this is also a passage in the Bible. It is a bigger sin in his eyes not fulfilling the plans he has for you than any other especially when you know God has put it on your heart to do it. I went through the fire, and he wanted me to write down my experiences and considering the recent uncovered corruption seen in the Department of Justice and the FBI I feel God is bringing this to our attention for a reason. No longer should we look the other way and be apathetic that "that's just how things are these days" but stand up for doing the right thing can be part of this new generation and a generation and culture that care about justice as our forefathers and earlier generations did. I know I'm not the only one experiencing this type of injustice and that there are thousands that are feeling the same way. If you are one of these bright lights then do not be afraid, share your story now and come forward. You might ask why my attorney and the states attorney made me go through this ordeal when they knew I should never have been charged. You would think my attorney would at least hate the injustice and do right by his client. What can I say about this man except that he was more interested in securing his upcoming pre-retirement position in the County Public Defender's office and I learned of his new position about a year later from another attorney. It all made sense to me and it's entirely possible he secured this position by what he did in my case and possibly others. He knew this cab driver should have been charged with Unlawful Restraint before we went to court never sharing this with me. He made a deal with the Prosecutor protecting the Police department that was clearly at fault. Their decision to move forward taking it to court instead of throwing it out was a miscarriage of justice and deemed **Malicious Prosecution**.

I think all our families over the last two hundred plus years have come to this country with the hope of a better life, but I do believe we bend over backwards to accommodate the illegal's entering our country and at our expense while most of the time ignoring their expired visa's if they even had one to begin with, voting in our elections not securing citizenship first and of course letting them walk on a felony as was my experience. It was apparent the cab company had much to do with how this all played out. As most of you reading this are aware if you listen to the news at all, they have been stating this for now many years but I lived this and wrote about this almost five years ago and even shared my experience with a high-level official proving it all to be true. Again, God does not make mistakes and is intricate in his planning and timing. This is no accident this is a clear message not about hate and intolerance but about justice for American citizens and let us not confuse this and muddy the waters.

The case was dismissed with prejudice. My attorney said that's what we should do and after I received the cab driver's statement I asked if I should sue for damages, he said it probably wasn't a good idea and I should just let it go and he didn't handle that kind of case anyways. I did decide to forgive which is my nature and put this behind me. I should not have done this, forgive yes but not just let it go as they all have asked me to do at one point or another. As I stated, I wasn't aware anything was on the internet about my ordeal let alone the article that was present courtesy of the local Patch. It is now expunged or so I am told and there is no record of any of this, but it was interesting that one officer that I know more recently said to me in jest that "it's always good to pay your cab driver." With this statement, it is obvious they can access my file which is illegal but commonly done and I am sure they don't have the cab drivers' statement in my file as they would certainly have a different opinion.

The next step even if falsely accused and exonerated, is to clear your record. This was not told to me by Bruce Wayne and I found it interesting that I was the one responsible for clearing my name when I was the victim. I was appalled that I had to pay yet again to erase this travesty of justice and yet again I am told that's just the way it is. No one who is found not guilty let alone a victim should have to pay for clearing your record; it is yet another moneymaker for the attorney's and the system of corruption. As I stated earlier, I recently had an attorney tell me that I didn't appear to be a victim as I didn't seem the type to back down. I stated to him at the time I had no reason to think that someone who took an oath to uphold the law would do just the opposite. I told him I am stronger and wiser now and I intend to make it known by sharing my story. I hope I hear from many others, as there is strength in numbers. I realize this is not an easy topic to discuss, being arrested, even if you're not guilty. There will always be the people thinking you deserved it, not asking for the facts or the other side of the story. Most just want to keep it quiet and erase it no matter what it costs them. This only manifests the problem in the system and contributes to the corruption. Most just want it to go away and I know as I was one of them that let it go only to regret it later. I hope with this writing more victims come forward.

As I waited to hear about my recent job opportunity, I was unaware the story of my arrest was on the Internet for all to see; no need to run a background check just enter the name and well read all about it as you have no rights if arrested. Before the Internet those arrests were pretty much secret except to Law Enforcement and those who read the paper and even then, you would have to look it up in the police database which most would not have known to do. Mug shots should not be published either and often they are shown on television on a slow news day. It is unjust to make this private information public except in cases where one is found guilty. To smear someone's reputation based on an arrest is wrong but there was nothing I could do except to wait and hire yet another attorney and pay yet even more money to get it expunged.

I did find an attorney specializing in expungement to draw up the petition of which she charged me as well a cool five hundred dollars. She was not very pleasant either as I had the impression, she thought I was guilty and not the victim. I had to keep calling her to get this expedited but once she finally read the case, I believe she reconsidered her judgment of me and gave it some attention. It was clear from her case that the cab driver should have been charged with Unlawful Restraint and the Court also should have been cited for Malicious Prosecution. When she finally sent the expungement request to the municipalities, it sat on the presiding Judge's desk for two weeks and this was in September for 2012. The woman at the courthouse who I spoke to didn't understand why it was taking so long but I believed at the time that the Judge did become aware of what the police, the prosecutor and my attorney had done.

As I stated I wasn't aware of anything showing up on the internet until I was turned down for the position, I was interviewing for in the Health System. Once the Human Resource department ran a background check it was over for me, not getting the job and my former boss and now CEO of this great organization was not taking my calls. They never said anything except they had selected someone else, so I never was able to tell my side of the story. I was mortified and never spoke to my former boss again as she didn't return my calls. Maybe she was embarrassed but did not give me the opportunity to explain or I believe she would have felt very differently and although I think she would have understood I don't believe she would have proceeded hiring me as again it was her career that she was not willing to jeopardize, much like the Police Officers wanting to keep their jobs by staying silent. This was the first of many jobs that I was offered after going through the interviewing but then subsequently denied after the background check. I have had my reputation destroyed and it continues to this day and many who could do something about it think little of this.

Out of everything bad there is good and through this potential job I did meet a wonderful man who would have been my boss had they offered me the job. He was a devout Christian, highly educated, and highly regarded. On my first meeting with him he gave me a copy of "My Utmost for His Highest" by Oswald Chambers. I knew then that this man was one of God's chosen coming into my life even for a moment helping me even in sorrow. I read this daily, and it taught me so much and gave me strength to move forward. I still refer back to his teachings today and have given this book as gifts to many. I intend to send my story to him, I wonder what he will say.

The Internet

Does the Internet need to be monitored? Some say no but, many have been hurt by untrue stories and private pictures with little recourse. I am told the attorneys have captured this market as well so why would they want the internet to be monitored when they can make a fortune representing all the obvious cases. It took months to get the patch story down as I needed a written document granting the expungement from the judge for this awful reporter to take it down. The incident happened in March, and I didn't get the story taken down until December, nine months later.

In any case not only was I attacked, terrorized, ripped off and maligned but I had little recourse as I tried to find an attorney, but not may attorneys go up against another attorney especially if they are connected; it's not done. These people have taken oaths to uphold the law and yet they break it all the time. They are no better than many of the guilty criminals they defend but I am sure these criminals never had the opportunities that these professionals have had growing up; shame on them and shame on sensationalized journalism. The "fake news" phenomena maybe aren't just manufactured to malign the Trump administration as this happened to me in 2012 and then it was whatever sells … even if it's free in the local news patch! We have and are more readily now experiencing a blatant lack of professionalism from many of our news channels and our reporters. Many report on what sells, not the truth, they edit what is said and change accordingly. It is incredible that they can put any story out there if you are arrested but they will not print a retraction with the real story. Yes, you can take them to court but, in this state, you will only spend money trying and ultimately you will not win, at least that is what I have been told and told to just let it go. I tried.

CHAPTER 7

THE MANY FACES
OF CORRUPTION

Before I was cleared of this injustice, I did secure a job in the beginning of June as the Director of Marketing at a company just north of my home. My first inkling was not to take it as my intuition is always dead on, but I wasn't having much luck finding other jobs with my name coming up as a felon as soon as they did a search; the byline alone of course got more people to click on it and look. How I had heard about this job was again quite my chance, but it did seem and upon further reflection that I was in a season of encountering the dark side and all that it implied. Earlier in the year I had made an acquaintance with a very outgoing and fun woman that was currently the HR Director at this company. She said they were looking for someone with my background but did warn me the company was very different. It was a family-owned company with deep ties in the State. She interviewed me in June and then proceeded to go on vacation. I did not hear from her, but I did hear from the V.P. of Sales and he asked me to come in for a second interview. I met with him as well as the President of the organization and his sister who headed up a division of the operation. They hired me on the spot, and I started the following Monday.

What was odd is they never ran a background check or why they interviewed me and subsequently hired me when my HR friend was on vacation. At the time I felt only relief that I was getting a job and getting this behind me, but I did have that same feeling that I should not have accepted. But that is the lesson, isn't it? But on the other hand, God does lead you and I understand now how it all ties together. Upon my friend's return she did not question it as she was just happy, I was going to be working there with her. What I learned later is the President was an attorney and most likely knew all the details of what happened to me and probably thought he could use it to his benefit at some point, possibly representing me in a lawsuit; or he knew the attorney and he was covering from him, either way he never approached me about it. All I knew is they were willing to hire me, so I didn't question it and did little research on this company's reputation except that they were a family-owned business that had been around for over 40 years. It didn't take long for me to find out that this family operation was a bit corrupt. They supplied the entire State and Government buildings with certain machines, so it actually was a huge operation, but it was kept small on paper. They had a good number of illegals working for them and had other divisions within their organization. Please note that I did not go looking for this company, it presented itself to me, so I do believe God was putting me in the exact place he wanted me to be.

Here I was experiencing corruption for a second time within months of asking God to show me my purpose. It was funny in a way because I had always worked for such wonderful above-board companies. I was part of four buyouts and being part of a buyout does not happen often in anyone's career let alone being part of four and these acquisitions do not happen if the company is not worthy. I worked for some of the best companies and best leaders in this state and to this day I am still in contact with them. We were trail blazers, building major databases for Fortune 500 companies, housing pertinent data for marketing purposes allowing our customers to better target and serve their customers. It was a wonderful time to be in business and I thank God every day for this opportunity that as a woman I never felt the discrimination that is apparent today and I felt only valued for my contribution. I could have asked any of my previous bosses for a job, but I didn't want anyone to know my circumstances. The shame stops you, keeps you in the dark and yet another reason to bring it into the light.

In any case my new employer had been in business for years and now with the aging owner in poor health the children of this organization stepped up to the plate, reluctantly I believe. I do feel that it was part of the family trust agreement that they could not sell the company while the father was still alive. It didn't take long for my friend as well as three others in the organization to open up to me about the corruption inside the company. They were quite open about it and I kept feeling they were telling me so that I would do something about it. Again, I had this great insight but once again failing to recognize it or in actuality, recognizing it but just failing to do something about it. God is good and thankful he forgives our oversights, our fear and our lack of faith.

Working for him gave me such an uneasy feeling when around him and I often felt he was the devil himself. I know God doesn't give you anything more than you can handle and I always felt God was with me but it was not easy, especially after what I had gone through just a few months earlier. At the time I wasn't aware that this was possibly God's plan, to have me experience so must evil and injustice now over the last ten years but you experience life going forward but unfortunately understand it going backwards.

Throughout June, July and August I had this pending expungement hanging over my head waiting on the new lawyer I hired to do the write up and submit the documents to the court. She had no problem billing me up front as this is the only profession that gets paid before they do a job; they say they have to bill ahead of time in order not to appear they're buying a verdict. This is probably one of the inherent problems creating corruption at the very core. Having to pay to erase injustices is just one part of it.

My immediate boss Scott Rogers was very nice and very open to discussing the company to an extent. He told me employees working for them stay and never leave. He realized there were issues but he just told me to learn the business and he proceeded to take me everywhere with him. He was a good guy. I had consistently asked for a customer list which was standard for the Director of Marketing to have but it was not forthcoming. I wasn't asking for anything but their names and location but I was denied this information. While I waited patiently working at this interesting place I did meet some other honest people in the process. I already knew the Human Resource Manager and she spoke quite openly of the practices of this organization but I also heard from the Vice President of Finance and the Warehouse Manager. They all gave me stories of the illegal activity at this company. The Vice President is no longer at the company and this does not surprise me as she told me she was looking to get out as soon as she found another position. The warehouse manager is still there as far as I know and my conversation with him was by far the most interesting and enlightening conversation I had while working for this company. He was a young Hispanic and as he himself stated, willing do anything. I asked him how he attained this job and he said that "the two sisters in the family loved him and they gave him the opportunity." I didn't know what that meant but let's just say that's not a good reason to keep someone on especially if he is divulging company information. We met a couple of times outside of work and he proceeded to explain how the warehouse operated as there was more than just the company product in the warehouses. When I left the company, he said I was too good for this company.

The Finance manager was relatively new as I was and highly credentialed and attractive which didn't surprise me as I believe the boss liked being surrounded by attractive women. She told me they would allow her to enter information into the books but then they would take them from her and lock them up. Nothing was online which was odd. They also secured the entire complex at four o'clock pm every day utilizing gates and padlocks, unaware of this I almost got locked in the first week of my employment. The HR manager was very vocal about all the illegal activity concerning the employees and their hours and their pay. She told me she informed Clark Rodney on a regular basis, but he just ignored her and didn't have to worry about such trivial things; it was very apparent his connections were long and deep. He was sued a few times based on what available information is out there but as I explained if you don't have the money, you won't get a positive verdict, and these were obviously from a lower economic status or most likely illegal in this country. They all had their stories but were relinquished to stay as most had been there for years. The IT Manager disliked me due to my questioning him on some of the sights and basically making him do his job. I found out later he was fired from this company for his attitude but subsequently rehired because he threatened to expose them, and it must have been something highly damaging.

In any case, I continued to do my job never getting a budget from my boss or never getting the client list either. As far as offices, we the humble servants were on the warehouse side while the Royals had luxurious offices far away from us on the other side of the facility. I was summoned there frequently by him. I must say his artwork was impressive as well as his real estate dealings. There was also a murder on the facility, but most people didn't talk too much about it. I realize how odd it is that these people confided in me. I do believe they wanted me to do something, anything. I didn't really know what to do at the time not understanding where God was leading me so I decided to be quiet, wait for the expungement and then I would look for another job. I would get it all behind me but just know God may have other plans for you and in my case he did.

I continued to call the County courthouse to check on the status of my expungement. The clerk was very understanding and did admit it was unusual for it to take so long for him to approve which again started me questioning what was standing in the way. I only hoped the Judge was thoughtful, wanting to do the right thing based on all the wrong I had experienced. I don't know the answers to these questions, and I probably never will but I can't shake the feeling to this day that Clark Rodney knew what was going on as he quite often reminded me that he was an attorney and very powerful in this state. I continued to work for them updating their website and putting a marketing plan together, but I think he knew I was on my way out not wanting to work for his company.

We spoke regularly of his coffee line which the division was not here in the states but in South America. He wanted to expand the line and spoke of soliciting other attorneys to buy his product and have it in their offices for their clients. I agreed it was a great idea but told him it could also work for Insurance companies and even Financial Institutions. He gave me a listing of all the attorneys in various areas and wanted me to email them the offer. Part of my marketing plan was to create an email solicitation program to increase their customer base for their coffee business but by law you can only solicit existing customers and as often as you like but soliciting new customers requires purchasing those names and adhering to solicitation rules and opt in agreements. Now I am sure some companies don't adhere to the rules and take a chance on getting penalized, but I was not willing to jeopardize my career and to this point a stellar reputation. I explained the process to him which I'm sure he already knew and well he just smiled and said it wouldn't be a problem and to just proceed. Thinking back maybe God was testing me to see if I would succumb but I held fast and being the professional I tried to keep him on track and use proven and legal means to that end and kept delaying the solicitation.

I stayed quiet in response to anyone sharing any further adverse information and started going out for lunch so I didn't have to hear anything more, but it didn't matter they would come into my office, sit down and just share. It was not a good experience and I just wanted out. Still, it did keep coming to mind there must have been a reason they were sharing this information with me. Again, I have learned to take heed to these experiences and not discount them as God always has a purpose in every person you meet, every word that they speak and every experience on your path.

As I stated he earlier had instructed me to take the names and addresses right out of the local Law directory that he handed me; he wanted me to solicit lawyers of all people by email! Considering this I am now praying pretty much every minute of the day asking for guidance and asking why I was once again put in another horrendous situation, and it appeared I was being tested. Since it is illegal to solicit via email, I sent him the following email explaining why I could not.

> In regard to the status of the email blast to all your legal professionals I did want you to know this directory is not permission based and they have responded that we cannot use the names but did include a contract and price list to purchase opt in names.

> As you know if they are not permission based, we can get sued under the Spam Act or at the very least get black listed which will hold us up for a long time which could affect our solicitations to our current customers. It can be a domino effect. We will lose our license with our email blast provider if I load and send non-permission-based email addresses. They take this very seriously. In my opinion it is not worth the risk. Please advise.

He never replied to my email, and I also feel one of the longtime employees who embraced this company's business practices had gone to him explaining that others were sharing information with me about the business and their obviously illegal activities and again, I need to reiterate I did not seek this information from anyone at this company, they came to me.

On **Thursday September 27th** the Presiding Judge in my case finally granted the expungement and on **Friday September 28th** I was fired from CB Account. Coincidence, I think not and not surprising once again my friend, the Human Resource Manager was out of the office. I was hired while she was on vacation, and I was fired while she was out of the office. It did not surprise me, but it was just so blatant, even for this powerful man and although this is an at will state for employment most employers are cautious firing someone especially when they have passed their ninety-day probation period, if you are over forty years of age and you have in writing their requests asking me to do something illegal. It obviously didn't touch him.

After working for so many exceptional companies I believe I was being shown the other side of the coin just so I would be prepared. I had heard of the corruption in this state but unless you experience it firsthand most people don't bother themselves about it. They talk about it and maybe even joke about it, conceding that's just the way it is here but this is a very dangerous apathetic position to hold as it just breeds further corruption thinking the people of this great state don't care. What I did find out is that some people in this state are untouchable and he is one of them. It's all about the connections. But there is a higher power, and those connections have a way of dissolving when there is enough evidence and someone will be offered up, case in point the arrest of a very long-standing alderman and a certain department head of a county prosecutors department here in this state, and we shall see if there are more. I believed the judge had done the right thing and finally approved the expungement after weeks of it sitting on his desk. Now, one could and really should ask shouldn't he have gone farther and asked for an investigation; maybe he did and that was causing the delay.

CHAPTER 8

THE FATEFUL DAY

The next step in the expungement process is the State Police clearing your record. The woman at the County office warned me to not call the State Police as they wouldn't like it and I thought this was odd as they are here to serve and protect and really didn't know what she meant by that statement. Possibly they thought I had paid my way out of it as so many do and I can only guess that they see so many clearly guilty people getting their names cleared that it may adversely affect them and I can see both sides and I can understand their frustration but the police officers I now know would not have condoned these specific officers' behavior that night nor would they have condoned the court prosecuting me as I was the clear victim and continued to be victimized. I made the mistake and did call them against her advisement, and she was right they didn't appreciate hearing from me. I left a message on Monday, and they called me back on Tuesday and please know there is a record of these calls. It was a female officer and she had little time for my questions, as was apparent by her tone although confirming she had received the order to expunge. The conversation ended abruptly with her basically, hanging up on me when I asked when it would be completed. So, I spoke to the State Police on Tuesday afternoon and just a little over twenty-four hours later I was pulled over by a patrol officer on a state highway. This was not a coincidence that I waited on the judge for weeks, finally getting an approval, within a day I was fired for not doing something illegal for this well connected and powerful attorney and then get arrested the day after speaking to the State Police about my expungement.

I am certain Clark Rodney could easily orchestrate this just by calling in a favor and he was very thorough in everything he did and well getting arrested will pretty much discredit one if you're contemplating a lawsuit against your employer for unlawful termination

This all took place in less than a week and was no coincidence as many others wanted me to believe. It's easier for them to manipulate you into believing you were guilty and deserved it or tell you that you are overreacting telling you to just let it go rather than have them open an investigation into these deemed important people of this state.

This police officer worked the midnight shift and was known for profiling but I also felt he was waiting for me on this state highway. He turned on his lights as I took a right turn into a subdivision, but he never turned on his camera. There was no valid reason for pulling me over he just stated that I had crossed the median even though he couldn't have seen me do this as there are no medians on this road and in the transcript the officer under oath stated I did not signal when taking the turn, so right away there were two different stories. One other theory is the officer ran my plates as I drove by him as he was parked on the left side of the road, found the not yet expunged dismissed charge and decided I was a good candidate to be pulled over. Actually, if I was an officer, I probably would have done the same thing but it is actually illegal for them to do this type of profiling without cause.

I did have a passenger in my car and a witness to this abuse of power as I was giving her a ride home as she did not have a car. I assumed she had cancer because she always seemed to have medical issues, but I did not pry. When we were pulled over, she stated that I didn't do anything wrong but before she could finish her sentence, she was asked to get out of the car by two additional officers that had arrived at the scene. They proceeded to physically search both of us as well as my car and our purses. This clearly was not warranted, and a violation of our rights called illegal search and seizure. I later found out he didn't have his camera on, so it was not documented; again, not protocol but you don't want to document illegal activity do you and this was after all 2012 and they were not held to the standards they are today.

Hesitating to trust any officer at this point and after the cab incident I told them I would not blow into their apparatus but that I would give a blood test and requested they take me to the hospital. This was not granted. As Bruce Wayne my attorney in the cab incident stated sometimes bad things happen to good people. I agree but it needs to come out and the authorities need to take responsibility for their actions as they had absolutely no cause to do this as I was not under arrest, nor did they have cause to go through my purse which was closed and located in the back seat on the floor. The police report said the prescription drug bottle of my thyroid medication was in plain sight but that was not true as it was in my purse. I did also have two empty bottles in the glove compartment along with my neighbor's prescription that she had left in my car at least six months earlier and never asked me for it. I later found out that she went on a lower dose, so she never inquired about her prescription. They knew it was not mine, but they decided to charge me with possession since it was considered a controlled substance even though it was indeed my neighbor's prescription later giving a deposition confirming this.

They took me to the local precinct and the next twenty-four hours no one should have had to go through. Being the honest person and still trusting in the system I told them of what I had just been through with the cab incident and its expungement which they should have investigated before further victimizing me. If he was not instructed to pull me over and I do believe this to be the truth, then I can only assume he thought I was lying and I was one of many that paid my way out of a situation as many do. I can understand what officers are up against; they make an arrest and then they get thrown out based on whatever the "good lawyers," prosecutors and the judges agree to. There are the honest cops but what I was told about this arresting officer was an entirely different story as it seems he had arrested over one hundred people over the last few months working the night shift and was named officer of the year in February of 2013 by his superior. He would make arrests at night and would spend his days in court collecting time and a half and possibly other favors and this is what I was told by an attorney that knew this officer quite well. He was known and it is my understanding he was promoted to Detective not long after my case.

They never got the details on the cab incident, so they didn't give me the benefit of the doubt and again they were not following protocol and put me in a cell for the night. They proceeded to open and slam the door every five minutes so I could not sleep, not that I probably would have based on where I was. They did allow me one call, so I did call a friend and left a message to meet me at the courthouse the next day. They finally took my picture at around five o'clock in the morning after I had been awake now for over twenty-four hours. They transported me to the courthouse in chains with my wrists handcuffed to a leather belt that was wrapped around my waist. I was told this should never have been done but it was. I did not call an attorney because I didn't know any other attorney except Bill Wayne, and I would never have called him based on my last experience. I probably should have which now I feel was a mistake not to. I opted to talk to the public defender, again still trusting the system and thinking the best of people expecting him to straighten this out but he never even met with me, and I was just brought in the court room, meeting him for the first time as we appeared in front of the judge. The prosecutor did state I had no previous record so obviously they confirmed the expungement, but it didn't seem to matter. I do believe they wanted to insure I would not bring a lawsuit against the police department in the cab incident; charging me with this only solidified my apparent guilt in the previous case.

I had a friend at the courthouse with the money to bail me out, but she later told me she kept asking them where I was, but they would just say they didn't know yet. Right after the court appearance I was sent back to a holding cell where I kept asking why I was still being held. One kind officer did tell me they were taking me down to the County jail and he didn't know why. So once again my rights were violated, and I was taken downtown to the County Jail in a Police wagon chained together with two other women. I realized soon after why the prison guard upon arrival at the courthouse had asked me my name and proceeded to put a red "X" on my hand. She stated that if I had someone bailing me out, I should not wipe it off, when in reality the 'X' signified I was to be transported to the County jail with previous convicted felons but also with the possibility of innocent victims as well or sad to say possibly the many homeless or those with drug addictions. Now you may say this is pretty incredible, but it all happened. I just don't know why they were violating my rights in so many areas but most likely the answer was "because they could!" This was not protocol for a first offense, no proof, no prior record, and a witness professing my innocence on top of it. Every attorney I spoke to told me this was so wrong and really unheard of but it mattered not and in reality, I have found this happens more often than not and they use it as a way to intimidate and instill fear in a person causing them to pay their way out of their circumstance rather than fighting for their rights, not wanting it to ever happen again.

The trip down to the County Jail was terrifying as I was not alone and as I said was handcuffed to two women. Both were young and one of was obviously ill as her hands were becoming three times the size they should be because her cuffs were too tight. She was a big girl and proceeded to vomit on us and they did nothing to help us we just had to sit in it the hour it took to get there. We were not allowed to clean up even after getting to the jail. Upon arrival, we were lined up next to each other and once again had our pictures taken. We were allowed to make one call and I called my Niece who lived in the city at that time. This was at noon, and I was not released until nine o'clock that night even though she paid the bond at two o'clock that afternoon and heard nothing as she waited for me to be released. I did not receive anything to eat or drink and there was one water fountain in the jail cell that did not work and a toilet that all could watch. The guards proved to be useful as their role was to open the jail door every ten minutes and slam it shut, basic harassment but I must say it was effective in unnerving you especially if you have been up for over twenty-four hours.

After several hours hearing women scream and curse, we were transferred to another area to be examined by a physician. I didn't want anyone touching me and they did not force me. They then requested we give a urine sample, which I did as I was not worried but the one girl that I came down in the wagon with was not complying and after an hour of this the guards stated we were not going to get any food until we all complied so since there were obviously drug offenders not willing to get tested, we received no food, basic extortion. This was against our rights as well as it was inhumane as there were two pregnant women that did not receive any food or water and I'm sure this was not an isolated incident. Really is this what our system is; basic human decency is and was not present? I would challenge the current Sheriff, who has been so vocal and even heard on certain National news programs professing to be so concerned with the inmates in this county jail that are wrongfully convicted, mentally ill and those incarcerated just because they cannot post bail. I wanted to tell him basic respect is not demonstrated in the processing of those arrested but not even found guilty. I was shown this firsthand for a reason and as I stated this was no accident, God entrusted me with this information and subsequent information on corruption in the following years and he will not let me keep it in even though I would rather forget as anybody would.

My niece posted bail for me at two o'clock in the afternoon and I was not released until nine o'clock that night. I had now been awake for almost forty hours and the ride home with my niece was a long one and she couldn't believe what I had been through. Even after knowing all this and many years later she tells me on a regular basis to "stop poking the bear!" I had never heard this before and find it quite comical and to this day it still makes me laugh when she says it. I do agree with her it does make sense to not further aggravate a seemingly unwinnable situation going up against such powerful people but when God wants you to follow through you just need to be brave and tell your story. Those that are part of this blatant corruption, well they're the ones that need to "stop poking the bear" as the bear is the man upstairs and he will not tolerate their corrupt ways much longer.

Please note this was in 2012 and look at the various agencies today coming under scrutiny for their illegal behavior and the many changes made this year. Those that corrupt the law will be held accountable as one can see how this is now playing out both in our State Government but also in our Federal Government. Bending the rules, obtaining favor and obstruction of justice will not be tolerated by the people. The people have been awakened from their slumber and the embedded officials through their attacks and diverting attention is not going to work as God knows all and sees all. The people need to take back their country and those that have been in office too long, well times up and becoming a lobbyist after being a government official well that dog don't hunt either and is and always has been criminal let alone a conflict of interest. Knowledge of how the system works, developing incestuous relationships for favor should not be tolerated. This has only corrupted our system making a handful of people wealthy while working part time on the issues and the other on their own special interests. The honest ones, well you know who you are, and you know what you must do. I believed God is giving us another chance and prophetic maybe but all I know for sure is that I am only a vessel he is using filled with his message. Maybe nothing I say will make a difference but that is not for me to determine, it is his determination.

CHAPTER 9

THE ATTORNEYS

That weekend I was referred to an attorney by a friend who knew him from a family connection. I met with him the following week and he was nice enough, but he took calls throughout the entire meeting, smoked cigarettes and told me it would be thirty-five hundred dollars to get a supervision ruling and drug school, he said the drug charge was ridiculous and it will be dismissed. I told him I was not guilty so why would I accept this plea, he said we could talk. I was still stunned although I shouldn't have been after going through my last attorney. And by the way you can ask yourself how did he know what the ruling would be if he just met me? Stunning to me and I hope to you. They are not interested in justice they are interested in what the market will bear in other words how much you are willing to spend for a not guilty verdict. Now this is the case even if you're clearly not guilty, even when they have the knowledge and proof that police failed to follow protocol and have violated your rights and the mere fact that you have witnesses to corroborate your story. They especially like the fact one is educated, employed, and pretty, at least under a male judge. I was told I would not be seen by a woman judge as I would not get a fair trial. Unbelievable, all he had to do was prepare a motion to quash and this case would have been thrown out, but then no one would make any money, would they?

After I was introduced to lawyer number one and was not impressed, I was given the name of an attorney that was supposedly a good guy that was a friend of a friend. I thought I could trust a friend but again I later found out that "friend" and "good lawyer" just means they are connected, know the system and how to pay your way out of your trouble. This was not my intention as I didn't need to, I just needed them to listen to me and have them make a motion to dismiss. Most "good lawyers" are previous prosecutors with the States Attorney's Office, and they know how the system works because they were part of it. They get good rulings because they know the people and how they are all connected. They also know who to go to as far as the police, whether it is the arresting officer or maybe even his superior. They may be on the take themselves or they may be honest and asked to change their testimony as a favor; it is done. He suggested I talk to a man named Larry George; now remember this is not his real name and I was only told that he knew a woman that worked with this person at a local store and that he represented her husband a few years back. Her husband was a city Fireman which sounded even more reputable in that he was helping a city employee and a man willing to protect our lives.

I have since found out that he represented many of these workers and not necessarily because he was a great guy but it was a lucrative business and the judges don't usually want to find these government workers guilty. I was given a phone number for him and was told his office was in my own town down the road not far from me which made me feel even more comfortable. I decided to drive by and see his office but when I got there the door was open and the offices were being worked on by some contractors, actually it was being totally gutted and redone. They told me that this firm that Larry George owned had been kicked out of this town and he had since moved to another town. The offices reeked of smoke, and I had such a feeling of dread when I was talking to them although they were very polite and after all they didn't have to give me this information. The last time I did not heed my intuition I regretted it and the feeling was no different. I just think that God gave me this gift and me being human I did not honor it or really understand it yet. I do not make this same mistake anymore. But out of everything bad God will make it right and he probably already knew I would make the wrong decision, but maybe only then and now it becomes the right decision as it caused me to experience the system even further and gave me further insight into the corruption.

My first meeting with him was in his new office where I also met his partner who was smoking in the building right in front of me and cared less that he was violating an ordinance. I wish I would have done my homework on this law practice but when you are going through this you just expect you will be taken care of after all that is their job to support you, but this is not always the case and my advice to all hiring an attorney, always do your homework. If you are guilty and looking for a way to pay your way out of it there are those attorney's available but if you are not guilty or just an honorable person and want your day in court and justice to prevail well there are those attorneys that will represent you and by the book. They may not be rewarded in this world, but they are rewarded by doing the right thing. I commend those attorney's as well as prosecutors, judges and officers that strive to do what is right in this corrupt world but, they have taken oaths to do just that. The corruption should be the exception not the norm that is how it gets away from us and manifests itself going from bad to worse and complacency is the enemy.

In my first meeting with Larry George, he asked me to tell him what happened as he was clearly working on something else while I told my story. He never responded with any statements telling me what was legal and what was not legal. He never mentioned the motion to quash, he never mentioned they had no right to pull me over, he never mentioned that they had no right to search my car, to charge me or to abuse me taking me downtown in chains. Hearing of the previous cab incident he seemed at least interested but never even said he was sorry it happened to me.

He stated his fee was $2,500 and he said he would see me in court and bring a check with me. I didn't understand what he meant as I just paid him the $2,500 up front but I would soon find out how the extortion game works. You see once you are "in" to an attorney for so much money changing attorneys will cost you even more and you don't know they won't do the same thing as the last attorney. You just keep praying it will end at some point. It may for some it didn't for me and every month he kept asking for more money and when I asked him about his original fee of $2,500, he stated that he told me that was his retainer which was not true. Now please understand these "good attorneys" never put anything in writing either. They don't leave emails and they rarely leave voicemails unless it is to tell you he will meet you at his office, change a court date or he is running late which he always was. He also changed who I should make out my checks to which after some research I found out was a not-for-profit company that he owned. My check became a contribution; tax free and he knew I would not be found guilty, so this was a good case for him. So not only was he to make substantial money on an innocent person but he also claimed a nonprofit status allowing him to not pay taxes on this income. Early on my feeling was that he wanted you to believe you were indeed guilty of the charge so that he could justify his exorbitant fees and as well be your hero getting the accolades when he gets you an acquittal. He was very good at what he did meaning he was well connected and not the brilliant defense lawyer he so wanted me and the world to believe.

My original court date seemed to be an apparent conflict for him and although he left me a voicemail message telling me he tried to change it he said the prosecutor Clark Michaels denied his request giving no reason. I didn't at the time hear the reason for the denial to move the court date or even know why he wanted it changed but was later revealed to me that Larry George knew the judge and due to their association, it was a conflict of interest for her to preside over the case. Being the daughter of his current law partner, created a clear conflict of interest and at the hearing Judge Marie Jill did not recues herself even though that is what she should have done. The second evidence he didn't play by the rules was when asked by the judge if he had filed a motion to quash and he stated that he had not but of course would. She allowed the case to be heard and after hearing from the Police officer who by the way had totally changed his story basically exonerating me; she allowed my case to go to trial stating that had Larry George motioned to quash she would have possibly made a different decision. I am assuming not wanting to appear bias she let the case against me proceed. We also appeared before her a month later where she obviously did not recuse herself once again and once again, she did not ask whether Larry George had filed a motion to quash which she had mentioned in the first court date. I wonder now how many of his cases she heard, and it would be interesting to know but I believe that information would not be available even through a FOIA request.

The police officer, under oath stated he had no reason to pull me over but, in this officer's, original report, it stated I had crossed a median that did not exist but in his written statement he stated I made an illegal turn. This is all in his original report and the transcript which I have both in my possession. Larry George had obviously gotten to this officer already starting his defense of me, as it was so scripted. Also, the original plea deal of supervision and dismissing the drug charge was no longer on the table. I was given no choice but to proceed with a trial and when I asked him about this, he responded to me "well you're not guilty right? "I of course said yes to this master manipulator and the conversation was over at least that day. I knew I should have found another attorney but at this point I really felt there wasn't one on earth I could trust and, knowing now what I knew of Larry George, there wasn't an attorney that would even take my case, not wanting to go up against him.

For I know how many your transgressions are and how great are your sins you who afflict the righteous, who take a bribe, and turn aside the needy in the gate.
Amos 5:12

I was directed to appear once each month for the next three months, him asking for continuances so that he could get the judge of his choice therefore insuring a not guilty verdict. That's how they do it legally as they wait until the presiding judge that would normally hear these cases goes on vacation. He wanted a specific judge and do remember he told me I would not get a fair trial from a female judge, again such manipulation. I didn't know this to be true but after doing some research on her I believe she would have demanded he file a motion to quash and then his case would have been over. Judges need to rule on the facts and impose outcomes on the evidence. It is apparent that many judges overreach their authority in many areas imposing sentences that are not standard for the crime, quite often very minimal sentences or dismissing them all to together for those obviously guilty but willing to pay much like the recent case now in the national news. You see this is how this illegal activity continues as even a non-guilty person is talked into being sure of getting an acquittal by paying for it although they will tell you there is no guarantee. The 402 Conference comes in to play here which should be illegal as these meetings between the judge, the attorney and the prosecutor are requested and deemed pertinent to the defense of their client, but they are not recorded and just a way to discuss the outcome based on negotiations of a monetary nature or at least favor based. I have found out more recently there are judges that do not participate in these 402 Conferences because they are not recorded. These Judges are the bright lights we need, and they should be commended.

As stated, Larry George never filed a motioned to quash with the court which the transcript states had he she would have heard more and based the evidence she would have had to throw the case out as it was an illegal search. Had she dismissed the case which she wouldn't have done; being associated with Larry George, it would have put her ruling in question, better to break the law denying my rights up front! Several months later I found the copy of the motion to quash while reviewing my case folder at the courthouse and it had a signature on it but it was not my signature, so it seems forgery is also an acceptable practice.

I found out over the months of interacting with Larry George that he did not like to be questioned and at one point the look on his face and his response to me caused me to be afraid of him. I found out much later from an attorney and previous prosecutor that he was known for his temper and at one point he was sentenced to anger management classes due to him assaulting another attorney. This was told to me in passing and again not a coincidence. It is interesting that all these things came to light after the fact but that is the lesson isn't it. As the months passed, I was required to continue showing up in court each month hearing his excuses for not proceeding as he waited for his selected judge and also while his fee kept increasing; asking him why he replied that he told me early on it would increase. This was not true, and that is why some attorney's do not sign a contract with you or correspond with you via email as it can be used against them should you file a complaint against them.

The chances of the two events happening to me within months of each other were not coincidence and not due to anything I had done that was deemed illegal. God has sustained me through the fire and never left me. Although hard to go through I know in the end it is worth it. God will vindicate us and punish those who wrong us and turn our bad circumstances around to benefit us in the long run.

"Even though you planned evil against me God meant it for good."

The one other fact I need to explain is how my neighbor's prescription came to be in my car and why she was never allowed to testify. She is the daughter of one of my neighbors at the time who also have a son who is a wonderful young Christian man. I got along with both and they seemed to like to talk with me and the parents, at least the mom was happy that I would give them good advice and tell them that their parents loved them even when it may not seem that way to them. She had gone off to college, gained weight and failed to achieve good grades so she came home. Her leaving home and attending college was an obvious stress on her and had taken its toll with the weight gain so since I had recently lost weight attending certain classes, she started going with me to meetings and she also hitched a ride when I was going to the gym as she did not yet have a car. She confided in me often and her parents were not happy that she failed to get good grades in school, but they were happy she was back on track. She got a job and decided to attend the local college. While attending she took an art class and one day presented me with a painting she had done, she said she was thinking about me the entire time while painting it so she felt I should have it. It is a picture of a black lamp post with bright yellow lights on the inside with bright red and yellow flames appearing on the outside. I didn't understand the significance of it at the time as this was spring of 2012 and I had just gone through the cab incident but in not too long I did realize its meaning as it is very telling and very prophetic. I call it my "Refining by Fire" picture and my Christian friends who have seen it are immediately awestruck, knowing its meaning and what it signified not even knowing my story. The Senior Pastor in the church upon seeing it had a different thought and said, "it must be wonderful to be a bright light to someone."

These trials will show that your faith is genuine. It is being tested as fire tests and purifies gold, though your faith is far more precious than mere gold. So, when your faith remains strong through many trials, it brings you much praise and glory and honor on the day when Jesus Christ is revealed to the whole world.
1 Peter 1:7

Larry George knew it was her prescription, but it seemed he didn't really want to address it or maybe more accurate is he thought he didn't have to address it but at my insistence he agreed to get a deposition from her. I should have known he was just doing it to keep me happy and to appear he was following the legal process as it was all for show. As she was just finishing up giving her deposition stating the prescription was hers, she got a call from her father while we were still at his office. I felt this was prompted by a call to the prosecutor by Larry as it was too coincidental, and she told me before the meeting that she didn't' tell him where or what she was doing. In any case after this meeting, she would not answer my calls and she was never allowed to testify. He stated she would not make a good witness of which I did not understand and told him so and as usual he got angry with me and told me to let him do his job. I should have known there was more to the story than he was telling me.

Several months later as has often been the case, God uncovered the real reason through her brother who was home on break from college. It seems in the summer of 2012 she had attended a party where she had consumed quite a bit of alcohol which I guess is normal for many her age and had gotten into an argument with her boyfriend and that he allegedly struck her but that she was unharmed and came home that night not thinking anything about it. Her father once he found out about it had other ideas and decided to sue this young man obviously due to his families' wealth. It is recorded she collected sixty-three thousand dollars from this young man's family in a settlement to drop her suit against him. God once again supplied me with the facts through this young Christian man, just reinforcing the truth concerning the corruption in our court system. My attorney lied and told me she wouldn't make a good witness when he had already spoken to the prosecutor on her case, and they didn't want to jeopardize the lawsuit even if it caused a clear violation of my rights. This is called obstruction of justice and I confirmed that Clark Michaels was the prosecutor on the case. Here you have yet another example of a young rich kid having his parents paying his way out of his circumstances and a young girl not taking responsibility for hers. She was backed up by her father who should have known better. This is the truth; she knows it as well as her father, my attorney, the prosecutor, the judge and now many other officials. I to this day believe her mother knows nothing about this. I should have told her, but I did hope her daughter would do the right thing as she was initially prepared to do, she has not come forward, but I will continue to pray she will someday.

CHAPTER 10

THE COURT DATE

It was now March of 2013, and we were finally in front of the preferred Judge Frank Thomas, as opposed to the presiding judge who was now on vacation. This is how an attorney can bypass court protocol and wait on the judge of their choice without any appearance of impropriety. I had gotten to the courtroom early that morning and before proceedings sat in the back praying to Jesus once again that he be with me and guide my steps. The Prosecuting Attorney, Clark Michaels had looked over at me several times and I do remember feeling that somehow, he didn't want any part of this; like he knew it would end badly for him. When Larry George started interacting with the Judge and requesting the infamous 402 conference, they acted like they didn't know each other which is so rehearsed but so necessary to mask any impropriety on their parts.

I found out at this late date that the original plea deal of supervision and drug school was off the table, no reason given but since he secures a verdict by other means; fee or favor it now makes sense but paying for or calling in a favor for a verdict is still illegal. The bottom line was this case from the beginning should have been thrown out and they all knew it they just had gone too far now so they had to proceed. As Judge Thomas spoke, I once again had a terrible feeling of dread come over me and I was not prepared for what was to happen next. I was asked to leave the court room after he asked for the 402 conference which was odd as they never

PERFECTED FOR THE PURPOSE

retired to his chambers the entire time I was outside the courtroom.
I know this conference never happened that day in court but was
agreed upon earlier by Clark and Larry and this may have absolved
Judge Thomas of any wrongdoing, but I have since found out he was
one of the most corrupt judges in this county. In any case I waited
outside as instructed but stood at the courtroom door. The Judge
never left the court room as he continued hearing cases. To explain
these 402 conferences are about you and include your attorney, the
prosecutor and the judge but you are not allowed to be in attendance
and the conversation is not recorded. It was refreshing to hear some
Judges do not conduct 402 conferences as they want no appearance
of impropriety, again I am assuming this but possibly they have other
reasons. In any case these conferences are suspect and just appear
a vehicle for all parties to agree not on innocence and guilt but the
"deal" or more appropriately "the amount." I had this confirmed not
only by an attorney but an agent from the bureau.

After about thirty minutes Larry George approached me
outside the courtroom and told me that the Judge was offering
what is called 1410 probation. He said it was not a conviction, but
he also stated we should go to trial. I asked why he not throwing
this case out based on the facts and he said he didn't know why
the judge ruled this way, which was another lie as he still had not
motioned to quash. While we were talking the State's, Attorney
came out to find out why we were taking so long. I do believe he
did not want to be part of it but people in high places were forcing
him, namely Larry George but I could be wrong on this, and he
may have been making deals for years. I heard my attorney tell
him that she's questioning the amount which I believe he stated
this to renegotiate the amount with the prosecutor, but he did not
comply. I didn't want to be part of this illegal game any longer and
was tired of the manipulation, intimidation, extortion and threats
and they both knew this.

They continued to talk, and he then came over to me and his
tune changed dramatically telling me that he knew I was not guilty
but this is the way we do things here. I believe he finally sensed

71

how adamant I was against what he was doing and tried to again manipulate me. It didn't work. I felt a sudden surge of power go through me. I can't say I knew what I was about to do but I had little power in not doing it that I know. We finally went into the court room and Judge Thomas asked for our disposition and my attorney stated we were going to trial. With this I spoke up and stated to the court that I was not willing to buy a verdict. I honestly don't think I had any control in not saying this. Taking a plea deal was not optimal but somehow, I knew that's what I need to do at least in that moment. Unless you are in this situation you don't know what, you are capable of. I can only say I was overcome by the Holy Spirit, and you need to ask yourself why someone would put themselves in a situation that would cause them so much pain when they had a way out. It was the right thing to do that is the answer.

It was a shock to all of them. I really felt they all were at a loss for words, especially the judge. I continued looking at him with a face that was of stone ... unflinching, knowing he had the power to end all of this but sadly he did not. I heard later they thought I was at a breaking point and not stable. I find this comical in that anyone questioning their illegal practices had to have something wrong with them. This was not true, and I moved forward not willing to continue in this obvious charade of justice. I do wish I would have called them all out on their illegal activity while in court that day, but fear silenced me or possibly God did save this fight for another day.

You therefore prepare yourself, and arise, and speak unto them all that I command you: be not dismayed at their faces, lest I confound you before them. Today I have made you a fortified city, an iron pillar and a bronze wall to stand against the whole land, against its officials. They will fight against you but will not overcome you, for I am with you and will rescue you, declares the Lord.
Jeremiah :17-18

I know quoting from Jeremiah and this passage will cause some to question that God really intended for this to happen. I can only say that is what I was feeling and that is how I was led. If it helps to answer this question you could ask why anyone would put themselves in this situation if they didn't feel compelled.

The one thing I would learn later that year is that there was no turning back once you crossed Larry George and as I was sitting in the courtroom waiting for him it became apparent that he was doing the paperwork on my case instead of the prosecutor, so he was dictating the fees that I was to pay the state instead of him. I'm sure the state was going to give him a kick back. I know it doesn't seem possible, but it was in his handwriting, and I know this because he handed it to me. After we left the court room Larry George would not even look my way but told me to sit away from him and wait. After awhile he finally came up to me, held out his hand and as he was shaking my hand, squeezing it tight and kind of twisting my wrist he said, "you owe me fifteen hundred dollars and just so you know you were part of paying for this verdict and I warn you do not go up against me." Now you can ask whether he had some kind of epiphany, a realization of what just happened in his dark world, and he got caught. I did have to agree with him in one sense had I continued with him as my attorney knowing he was paying for a verdict and what was going on in this court room I would have been just as guilty as he was and of course the rest of them. I did find out the reason for him offering me his hand to shake is that the corridors are all under surveillance, he knew this and so that not only was this handshake a warning to intimidate me but it was also for the cameras that we parted amicably; such deception and what a show.

You shall not fall in with the many to do evil, nor shall you bear witness in a lawsuit, siding with the many, to pervert justice. And you shall take no bribe, for a bribe blinds the clear-sighted and subverts the cause of those who are in the right.
Exodus 23:2

As I stated it also seemed someone had given him the authority to fill out the paperwork for my sentence. I to this day don't know why he was allowed to make these decisions it should have been the prosecution, and yet another illegal action. It should be no surprise that he gave me the max amount for everything and that it added up to $10,000 total after his fee. I would assume these funds would find their way into somebody's pocket. Not a coincidence but in his eyes, I'm sure justified payback for my disobedience to the great Larry George. He would have his revenge now and through the next few years but in the end, he would be held accountable for his actions as God is a just God and he sees all.

I was instructed to go to the probation office immediately taking my file and was then interviewed by one of the clerks. She immediately took off nine hundred dollars saying it was excessive and incorrect. Knowing what had happened in court as she was there, she kept looking at me and finally stated that she thought Larry George did not lose cases and then she proceeded to ask me if I knew who he was. I asked her what she meant and at this point she told me he was none other than Senator Charles Johnson's private attorney, the Senate Majority Leader in this State. Well, you couldn't get much higher in this state and it helped me understand why this was all happening, talk about being thrown into the fire, not starting small but going straight to the top. Again, had he motioned to quash this case never would have gone further but he saw me as a good candidate in my background, the case itself, making money and of course another win for his record of never losing. I believe going to court and the win is what he truly craved. He said he was a "Good Lawyer" which doesn't mean they do the right thing it means they identify the right people, the right time and the right price.

In my first meeting I was told I had to submit to a drug test on a random basis, which never happened as my probation officer knew I was not guilty and said that I did not have to come in and could mail my payment in. Also, on that first meeting I was on 1410 probation which is different than regular probation and not considered a conviction, but this too was to change in my file to regular probation which is considered a conviction and I was informed of this by my next attorney who would become a resource to me in understanding the corruption in this county.

I also think it was kind of fun for these men, to put a professional woman through the indignity of a trial as they all get very bored with their days and well this was not so bad, a shoe in case and a woman as well. I do believe more women have been in this situation than is reported and I equate this to what was in the news a few years back about some powerful men and their abuse of women, and women who should have come forward but did not. Again, most are mortified and just want it to go away as I did with the malicious prosecution case, not fighting for my rights. Some are willing to compromise as they have been told by their attorney's they can't guarantee a win and well "that's just how things are done around here," as if what they are practicing is legal, accepted maybe but not legal.

Within a few weeks I did send Larry George a letter along with my final check succumbing only based on his many verbal threats of what he was going to do to me if I didn't pay up and remember he never put anything in writing. Here is the letter I wrote to him, forgiving him but also praying he would turn around and do the right thing.

> I have enclosed a final check at your adamant request and in response to your threats. We both know this amount was never discussed or agreed upon but knowing what kind of man you are and knowing those that serve you; I feel little recourse but to comply. Yes, you are a powerful man in this state but just know there are more powerful than you and yet a higher power that is over all and at some point, you will have to answer for your behavior and although this practice of law you have perfected is accepted, it is not legal as we all know.

I forgive you Mr. George and I pray you turnaround and be the man God wants you to be as threatening women, taking bribes and buying a verdict does not make you a "gifted attorney" it makes you a felon and at the very least a candidate for disbarment.

CHAPTER 11

EVIL ENSUES

A week after my court date and fateful decision and praying to God for an answer I had yet another encounter that was again not by chance. I was at my local gym and a man who I had spoken to on occasion came over and sat next to me on the stationary bikes. This was not uncommon at this gym as many have gone there for years and well you do get to know people after a while, at least enough to have a conversation. I usually talked to him about healthcare as he had his own insurance company but as we were talking, he out of the blue asks me if I needed an attorney, you know for tickets and such. Wow I thought God has answered my prayers but after thinking about it I do believe what I had done in court that day to the infamous Larry George was a topic of conversation among the many attorneys and after all my picture was all over the internet. I said yes one can always use a good attorney, not getting a name and walking away thinking how odd this was. Within minutes a man who I had never met named Mike Joseph (again not his real name) approached me and hands me a bank deposit slip with an attorney's name, phone number and his own name saying he was referring me. I thought God had a hand in this and keep in mind I had never met this man before in my life and I have several people who can vouch for this. It did seem quite coincidental that this happened within a week after my court date. Maybe my actions at the courthouse were so out of the ordinary it spread to others which would not surprise me now knowing how incestuous they all are and how connected this man handing me this attorney's number was as well. Maybe he was in the courthouse that day with this attorney and said he recognized me from the gym. I don't know but I did decide to call this attorney and at least tell him what happened and at this point I was still expecting the good in man and he was after all bound by the confidentiality agreement which I now know these types of attorneys rarely adhere to. I do believe that God was guiding my steps through all this and even though one bad thing after another was happening to me, I still felt his presence leading me through it. I can't explain it any other way. Through my experiences I can now help expose the "way things are done" at this courthouse and hopefully through this other will come forward; that is my prayer at least as I am but an instrument as many of us are, some aware, some unaware but still important in carrying out God's plans.

This attorney was also a former Prosecutor in the States Attorney's office, and his name was Rich Stevens, and it still amuses me that the so called "good" lawyers as they call themselves are always previous states attorneys with all the connections. I spoke to him on the phone, and he was so pleasant and helpful it was a nice change from what I had experienced with my last two lawyers. He stated he was appalled by the proceedings and the events that took place in my case but in hindsight I do feel now that he had already heard all about it from possibly Clark Michaels, the prosecutor in my case or someone at the courthouse. The one thing I did know is he really didn't know how powerful Larry George was or what he was capable of, or I am sure he would never have taken my case. From a legal stance and his defense for me, he said he found my attorney to be ineffective and that he would enter a request to withdraw my plea but, in the meantime, he wanted me to do all the classes which I did not understand but do now. You see even if you're not guilty you still pay for the classes and the BAID instrument in your car that way everyone in this swamp gets paid. He called me later that week informing me he had submitted the withdraw plea, a document that I never saw until later that year when looking through my file. It is funny how things have appeared in my notorious file over the last few years; this County having a non-automated system until 2018 allowed this but since the human factor is still there any attorney can look at your file, put anything in your file and take anything out of your file and never sign in as even requesting your file. I am thinking that they could even walk out of the building with your file if that is what they wanted to do and or the states attorney gives it to them. This system works for them, and they aren't going to change in the most corrupt county, in the most corrupt state in the union.

That morning in May, Rich Stevens and I appeared in front of the presiding Judge Helen Kaye, and he stated his name for the record and his representation of me and asked to withdraw my plea. She granted his request immediately which was within her power to do so but to my surprise my attorney than spoke up stating that it was originally Judge Thomas's case. I don't know why he did this but hearing this she changed her ruling and stated she would not hear anything further. It was clear she wanted no part of it and after her ruling we were dismissed but my attorney told me to sit tight and wait. I believe at this point Rich Stevens was working in my best interest, but this was soon to change. I sat in the court room and waited for him while he handled his other cases but after about thirty minutes a very large man appeared in the courtroom and sat in the back which was nothing new as many people always entered and left the courtrooms, but this man did pique an interest in the state's attorney, Clark Michaels almost instantaneously. Within a few minutes Rich Stevens after conversing with Clark Michaels came up to me and told me they no longer wanted me to stay, and they were going to wrap it up for the day. I deducted he may have been another attorney or an investigator that they knew, he did look a lot like Larry George, but I honestly don't know who he was, but one thing was for sure, they weren't going to discuss my case any further, not while he was there. I do believe he was there on Larry George's behalf as no one messes with Larry George as I found out later, but for the record I would do it all over again. You see these attorney's have many on their payrolls, including clerks who get paid well for keeping them informed. There is one older man in the clerk's office that comes to mind.

At this point I was told to leave the courtroom and wait outside and after a substantial amount of time Rich Stevens approached me seemingly very upset and proceeded to tell me that the States Attorney's Office is handling this case strictly by the book and wanted me to sign an affidavit on what happened in the previous case and to testify against Larry George, council to this residing high ranking official in this state. He said he would discuss the details with me later, but I do believe he didn't expect this and this time he wasn't acting as he was clearly a little shook up at least that is what I thought, but he is a great actor as many of them are.

I did ask why he told her that it was Judge Thomas's ruling if she had already approved the withdraw request, his response was that we had to go through Judge Thomas but if this was the case what were we doing in her courtroom appearing in front of her and also this contradicted what he had told me in an earlier meeting that it was her courtroom, she was the presiding judge and she could take the withdraw plea. This is again the manipulation and deception these attorneys have mastered. In his defense it was obvious all feared the very powerful Larry George and now he may have found out why. I know this man that appeared in the courtroom that day was representing someone, but I am not sure who. If he represented Larry George, why would he want me to testify against him, I would think he would want it to go away but knowing Larry George as I do, his pride got the better of him and remember his last words to me were "you don't want to go up against me. And for the record I am sure Judge Thomas also had something to say about my case making sure it stayed in his courtroom.

I don't scare easily especially in the face of such evil. We are but a mist, here for only a short time and to serve our purpose. If God be for me than who can be against me? When asked again and again how I selected Larry George as my attorney they all seemed incredibly surprised that I didn't know who he was. Again, I had no reason to think anything about him as his name was given to me by a friend of a friend and if you run a search on the internet nothing comes up unless you know in advance how to search by a combination of names, in this case the Senator and Larry George, this produced the information on him that was of importance. The internet articles not only discussed their relationship he also represented the Senator's family members, namely his sons on several occasions and as well many city workers.

I think in the end Rich Stevens hated that he got involved in my case and I believe he regrets it even more than he ever expected. I will be honest with you I feared retribution from testifying against Larry George and shared this with Rich Stevens, but even so I gave him all the details as I had before and did agree to sign the affidavit and was prepared to testify against him but while at his office, he told me to think about it and we would meet later. I did eventually sign what I thought was the affidavit that was written based on my deposition, but he gave me only the last page to sign and when I asked him for a copy of the document, he said he would get it to me which he never did. I even have it in a text to him that I would be happy to sign it and another email asking for a copy after I signed it which he never complied to. His statement that I didn't sign it was once again a lie.

I believed at the time he did want me to move forward on testifying against Larry George, but I also believe he thought I would drop the case out of fear. Not wanting this he told me I was not going to appear in front of Judge Thomas but Judge Maria Ellen; her being a female I guess was supposed to calm me but once again we were going in front of a different judge which he stated was not possible a few months earlier. I overlooked it and did not question him as I just wanted him to file a motion to quash and have this case thrown out which is again what should have happened. I went to the courthouse that morning and Judge Ellen's name appeared on the wall outside her room as is usual, but the court room was dark and also locked. Much to my surprise and it shouldn't have surprised me; Judge Thomas was in the next courtroom about to hear cases. I decided to wait for my attorney in the vestibule hoping for an explanation but as I was waiting an assistant states' attorney came up to me and told me my case had been moved to Judge Thomas's courtroom. Now I had never met her and possibly she had my picture in my file to determine who I was but how did she know I was sitting in the lobby unless Rich Stevens had informed her? When he showed up, he acted surprised and a little upset that this was happening, again great actors these trial attorneys! He even had one of his friends from the Clerk's office walk by us and say to him "too bad Judge Thomas is here today; we weren't expecting him"! I didn't buy it and felt this was just another great ploy they had orchestrated for my benefit so that I would proceed with the withdraw plea, the deception and manipulation continued. Months later I found the motion to withdraw plea dated well before my court date, in my case folder addressed to Judge Thomas and not to Judge Mandel, which just confirmed he lied to me fully intending to put me before Judge Thomas where they could control the situation.

Appearing before him would absolve all of them and keep control of me and possibly bring Larry George down. Brilliant I must say, and I believe they all want to take out successful attorneys as its less competition for them but this and their intent I cannot prove I can only explain what happened to me and the circumstances surrounding my case. More likely however, it was to get me to withdraw my plea and once this was done, retry my case, which Judge Thomas stated would be that afternoon, find me guilty, possibly give me jail time and in essence take care of me. They have the power to do this and as powerful as Larry George was, I can see him orchestrating this to happen and fulfilling his threat to me to not go up against him, but again I cannot prove this, but I can prove what they did was illegal.

My attorney also right before we headed into the court room and after many meetings stated to me for the first time that things could go very wrong for me and felt even if I testified against Larry George and was granted the withdraw plea, I would never get a fair trial from this judge and most likely I would get sentenced to jail time and he would be within his rights to do so. I was shocked but confirmed once again that my own attorney was not representing my best interest but covering for his colleagues. When you are scheduled to appear before a judge you have no choice but to go through with it, so we proceeded. I asked my attorney what was going on, but he didn't answer me. I guess I could have called foul, but it would have just made it worse for me. I didn't feel anyone was on my side and I didn't expect my attorney to lie to me and to manipulate and orchestrate the outcome of a hearing, no one should.

As I appeared once again before Judge Thomas, I felt that incredible dread once again. He proceeded to inform me that should I withdraw my plea I will be required to testify immediately against Larry George in open court and that he is on standby to witness his accuser and we would immediately proceed to trial. He said that even if he granted my withdraw plea, in the new trial he could sentence me to up to three years in jail should I be found guilty. With no time to prepare this was a clear threat and they think nothing of using these scare tactics. Also, early on when Rich Stevens first contacted Clark Michaels about the withdraw plea his response was "why would she want to chance it?" Why would he say this when he knew all the facts of my case knowing I wasn't guilty? This I also have documented in a voicemail from Rich Stevens. Now I know you may say this is ridiculous and that I was ignorant, and I shouldn't have believed him but please know that Judges can do exactly as he claimed and they have done worse in this court system in this county.

At one-point Judge Thomas I believe knowing this was going badly instructed my attorney to discuss the case outside the court room with me. Once outside, my attorney reiterated that I should just keep the sentence as he wasn't sure I wouldn't go to jail. It was intimidation at its very core and evident he was now in on it or at least was not willing to do the right thing by his client. After praying and asking for guidance I decided to withdraw my request and be safe and once again save this fight for another day. I am glad I did because since 2013 I have accumulated so much additional proof of not only corruption in my own case but in the cases of so many others. In the end they said I was afraid to testify which was not true and by me not withdrawing my plea they couldn't say I was part of this illegal activity of buying a verdict which allows me to discuss it and report it as I have.

When people ask me or surmise, I must have been guilty to keep the plea deal and not chance it they don't understand or don't want to acknowledge how powerful these men were and how valid the intimidation and threats I was experiencing from them. Although it hurt me both financially and in my personal life it is what the Holy Spirit was directing me to do. I felt the Judge was visibly upset as we looked into each other's eyes but not enough to do the right thing once again which he could have at any time on this day and in the months that proceeded this, I can only assume no one, even Judge Thomas as powerful as he was wanted to cross Larry George. I did think of finding another attorney and actually contacted a few after this but I felt it would just be the same process of covering up and now I had experienced three corrupt attorneys over the last year that were supposed to defend me and secure my rights. I had several Judges that were at least guilty of looking the other way and as well two corrupt States Attorneys not doing their jobs and for the record, no attorney would touch my case, never returning my calls. This was to be the pattern even to this day.

After we left the court room as we were walking to the parking lot my attorney stated that we could go before the presiding Judge Helen Kaye once again and request her to commute the sentence. He told me since all my community work was done instead of two years we could ask now to rule that I have completed it. I asked him how he could do this and he said it's done all the time. So, we went to court once again and he wasn't charging me for it which I could say was his conscience, not representing his client the way he should have but succumbing to the powers at be. As soon as court was in session he was nowhere to be found. They were calling my name and since he was not present they went to another case. When he finally appeared, he did have a document in his hand which he handed to the clerk which was added to my file. I was to find out later it was a signed document by Judge Thomas shortening my probation to one year and I do have this in my possession. Now if I was guilty do you think Judge Thomas would have done this but it gave me clarity that the one they all feared was indeed Larry George.

After waiting which seemed like hours we were finally in front of Judge Kaye with Rich Stevens requesting a 402 conference with her of which prompted a resounding outburst from the original prosecutor Clark Michaels and which shocked most everyone in the courtroom. He stated it was not a new case and did not warrant a conference looking over at Rich Stevens and then Judge Kaye. He was so very adamant about this that the Judge denied my request while by attorney said nothing in response. This testimony is not however in the now doctored transcripts and actually Clarke Michaels is never mentioned as saying anything in the transcript and even though she denied my petition she did so note that there was a lot of talk surrounding my case which was a clear indication she wanted nothing to do with it but at least there is this admission from the bench.

As we left the courthouse, he knew how upset I was and told me that we can keep trying to commute my sentence and then have it expunged; he told me he did it all the time and she will eventually grant it. He responded to trust him and it's up to the Judge's discretion in these matters. So, they can commute your sentence at any time but it may take many attempts, well this indicates that this is not about justice it's once again about money because every time you appear the court makes money and of course the attorney makes money and possibly the judge.

As he was stating how we could go back to court and make this all right something once again came over me prompting me to do the right thing and not succumb to this corrupt system, his tactics and him any longer. I informed him that the man that referred me to him, Mike Joseph, was never a friend of mine and that I had just met him that day at the gym when he gave me his number. I don't know why I told him this but I felt he should know that everything he said to me for the last few months was now a liability to him. He shared with me how the system worked and in actuality showed me although I never took part in it. He was not pleased to say the least and I really thought he wanted to hit me but instead he told me to never contact him again. I never did until recently but he certainly made me pay for it by spreading the word to other attorneys not to talk to me. All attorneys have access to our files by name at least in this courthouse and they don't have to sign in which is illegal as then they are not held to the confidentially clause. I was told this by a very nice and very new employee in court records. He did say this was wrong but again that's just how things are done around here.

I was reluctantly in contact with Rich Stevens again a few years later as I feel God was giving him and others the opportunity to admit their mistake and make it right but in the short time however I did not follow up with him. In my situation the last thing you can do is trust the system as you have exposed them and they will do anything and everything to discredit you and divert attention away from their illegal actions. As I said word does get around as it is an incestuous bunch; those in the courtroom and as well the low-level employees that work in court records.

It is obvious to me years later and reflecting on the circumstances of my case that no one wanted to intercede on my behalf. I shouldn't have been arrested to begin with, they never took into account the cab incident which was Unlawful Restraint on the cab drivers part and subsequent Malicious Prosecution, no attorney ever filed the motion to quash, the first judge did not recues herself even with a clear conflict of interest, the second judge was part of the intimidation, the other judges looked the other way and they did not allow my neighbor to testify on my behalf because of another more lucrative case and even though she signed an affidavit. The prosecuting attorney knew all this information as did my attorneys and the Judge and it was clear it was acceptable for me to suffer an injustice then to jeopardize the reputations of so many others; I was expendable.

I decided to just move forward after a few months had passed contacting at least six attorneys who initially said they would take my case but after reading my file and most likely contacting Rich

Stevens they either texted me they couldn't help me or they just never returned my calls. I was told later by two attorneys I should have exposed it then. Not getting anywhere, I volunteered my services at the church and tried to find a job.

CHAPTER 12

THE PUNISHMENT

Explaining additionally what I went through with the various state agencies in relation to my sentence further exposes the corruption that exists and not only in our court system. I am not saying everyone who works within agencies are corrupt, but many are and I experienced them in every area; again, not coincidence but I'm fairly sure the many stories I am about to share were prompted by the very attorney's I so upset.

The first thing that happens to you is meeting your parole officer who says they are on your side while pumping you for information. Mine knew I was not guilty but basically said she had to go through the motions, and she also stated I didn't have to come in and that I could just send in forms every month along with my payment.

Per this state's law people charged, not convicted with DUI are subject to losing their license after thirty days for thirty days or so I thought. Also, you may ask if you are truly guilty why they give you thirty days before you lose your license. They will say you are not yet found guilty which is true, but the thirty days is really just an opportunity to secure an attorney to create your plan ... I mean your defense. Your attorney is by law bound to file a motion to quash especially when they have no reason to search your vehicle and your belongings, so that the Judge can determine if there is merit to the case, again this was not presented in my case and Larry George had no intention of letting this case go not when he could make money, knowing I was not guilty and as well secure another win for the record. He was very egotistical and if I were to see him again which will not ever happen, I would ask him how good of an attorney he really was if all he did was lie, extort money and intimidate his clients and secure a win not by his exceptional talent but by buying a verdict. I am assuming God asked him at some point and his answer was unacceptable.

Due to this blatant act, I did lose my license which starts a chain reaction of revenue for many, and I found this out after the fact and I hope by writing this I am helping others who find themselves in the same circumstances. I don't condone paying your way out of your troubles but if you are truly not guilty then you are entitled to the rule of law and the truth of the matter is my attorney which he is not alone; won his cases by appeasing the state agencies making them money, guilt or not. It doesn't matter if you're found not guilty; in the end the state and other agencies have already made the money off you, and you are not reimbursed unless of course you take it to court. Larry George was part of this process being so closely tied to the state. Now attorneys would say that they are entitled to make a living and I would say yes if they were following the law which all he had to do was motion the court and I would have been exonerated.

Being responsible for taking my mother to her various appointments as she didn't drive didn't matter as he told me I must get a letter from her doctor stating I was her sole provider for transportation of which I did. Within hours after sending, it to him he stated that it was too brief. I provided yet another letter from her doctor and he said that it wasn't going to work and blamed the States Attorney, Clark Stevens for denying me but I don't believe he even knew about it. He wanted me to lose my license not only because it made me look like a victim to the Judge when he defended me in court but also because all the other agencies get paid this way before you are found not guilty.

Through all God does sustain us through our trials, at the time it may not seem so but one of the biggest signs and comforts to me was that the entire month I was without my car it was sixty degrees and sunny most every day in a month that should have had below thirty-degree temperatures and snow; it was a gift. I was able to walk to the gym every day and I guess I was lucky as I did not have a job yet. I do think about what other people must go through … they lose their jobs because they have no transportation or they pay incredible amounts to get to their job and then of course their employer may become aware of it, ruining your reputation at your company. And let's not forget the ones that cannot afford bail and are kept in jail until their court date. They are exposed to every element and most of the time they lose their jobs and, they may not even be guilty. Recently criminal justice reform was passed, and we shall see just how this will work as there are now complaints of releasing many violent offenders as there is no longer cash bail. It will be interesting to see how they are going to clear the records of those first-time offenders as there are so many. Will they have to obtain an attorney and go to court once again? I am assuming yes, and it will once again make many attorneys large sums of money, not having to do much work as they already know the outcome.

Another sure money maker for the State are the administered tests assessing you as a risk and that you pay a large fee. I am sure these counselors are paid off as well and for all I know Larry George slipped her a couple bills to give a glowing profile of me at least while he was representing me. It is a racket in so many ways and of course many may want to demean you, but I did have a very pleasant woman knowing I had not yet been to trial yet. She acknowledged it was wrong, but it is their job, and they don't want to risk losing it.

There are also the outside Drug counseling agencies that are quite well organized, meaning corrupt. The class I had to take which lasted several weeks and cost several hundred dollars and was owned by a husband-and-wife team and although they were very nice, I'm sure they are compensated in various ways. On my first visit I met with the counselor's wife who not only took my information but proceeded to ask me who my attorney was which now makes sense as many attorneys have agreements with, and I can confirm at lease this company got paid under the table ensuring their clients were treated right or more possibly to overlook anything that the client did that maybe was inappropriate. At the second meeting the owner told me that to get a written recommendation from him costs another two hundred fifty dollars. I informed my new attorney Rich Stevens about the charge and at the next meeting this counselor started back pedaling saying that I had misunderstood him of which I promptly replied that I didn't think so and asked him what part he thought I misunderstood; he was not amused. Once again, Rich Stevens was again exposed through his own entourage of followers aka the bought and paid for.

What I found most interesting and quite comical is they would request urine tests of certain people in the group and one night I overheard a man talking to the counselor stating that he had smoked marijuana (this is when it was illegal) recently and asked if he could he take the test later. The counselor replied that he understood and assured him he would take care of it. This was said right in front of me and as I stated they are all very matter of fact about it. I was once again in a state of shock but did continue to take notes and knew God was making this all possible for me.

The extent of the corruption continued to be made known to me and this time it was the outside agencies that manage and own the facilities that install the alcohol monitors in your cars. What I found out is they will calibrate your monitor for a fee, meaning they will look the other way and change a positive reading for a fee and the costliest, and trust me it is done is placing the unit in your car but not hooking it up. In my case I did not take part in any of it and this service swapped out the existing calibrator in my car without my knowledge in the very last month of the unit being in my car. I knew they had switched the unit as I had taken a picture of the serial number on the unit when it was first placed in my car and of course I have the pictures of both the serial numbers to prove this.

A month before the unit was to come out of my car, I received a letter from the state indicating I had a positive reading. Not ever drinking and driving I of course contested it and why would I chance it especially one month before it was to come out of my car and enduring it for eleven months? I can only assume one of my past attorney's put them up to it or it happens to many others just giving more opportunity for a payout. I felt Larry George behind this as it did divert attention from their illegal activity by making me look guilty. When I called the company responsible for monitoring these tests which interesting enough is in another state, they checked my file within seconds and told me there was no record of a positive reading. I told her about switching out the machine and she said that is never done. I told her I had pictures of the two with their serial numbers. She put me on hold for about ten minutes and when she returned to the call, she said the reading was valid and there was nothing she could do. I can only surmise she was on the phone with Larry George, or his contact and they were not backing down at all even knowing I could prove it was switched. It's as if he wanted me to go up against him even with all the evidence I had.

In any case I sent a denial letter to the state, and they said I could appear in court to challenge it. They knew this unit was scheduled to come out of my car in a few weeks so miraculously I got an appointment to appear that week and another opportunity for the state and their employees to make some extra cash. Once again, I encountered the corruption in the system, and I have little doubt the attorneys were somehow behind what I am about to tell you. To many it may seem I am creating a conspiracy theory but do know making someone look guilty certainly diverts attention from themselves. I have the pictures of the two units so it would be hard to deny what they had done and no doubt the station that made the switch was well compensated.

I went to the state facility on my appearance date without an attorney, but I was hopeful that I would get heard and justice would prevail, but my experience did once again confirm what I already knew. When I arrived downtown, I was asked to fill out paperwork; to sit and wait but I was not there long when an older man approached me and told me to follow him while others ahead of me continued to wait. We proceeded to go into a private room where he told me to fill out a new form; when I asked why as I had just filled out the

PERFECTED FOR THE PURPOSE

same paperwork and turned it in at the desk; he replied to just do it. Filling out a new set of paperwork at first didn't make sense, but it was the was the only way he could take my case. He then asked where my attorney was, and I stated I did not need one. He was not happy, and this made it obvious to me he knew my past attorney by looking at my file and he also knew what kind of attorney he was; one that paid people off for their cooperation. I told him I was not guilty; had proof and I didn't need an attorney. At this point he turned on a camera told me to be quiet and began filming me. I told him I did not drink and drive and that the monitor had been replaced even though they denied it and showed him the pictures of the two units with different serial numbers. At this point he turned off the camera and again asked me if I had an attorney and then said that only then could something be worked out. I looked at him with a look I am told can be quite disarming and at this point realizing he was getting nowhere; he turned the camera back on and said he would make his decision in thirty days.

I found out his verdict in record time and of course he did find me guilty which added another ninety days of the unit being in my car, incurring more cost but a small victory as no money at least went to this extortionist or an attorney. The thing that totally amazes me is that they are so blatant and exhibit little fear of being exposed; they appear to be untouchable much like the many I had already encountered. Again, the amount of corruption is in every area. Now I'm not going to say all attorneys pay government employees off, but it is obvious it is commonplace in this county and if your practice is in this area and you don't succumb to following illegal acts well you won't be very successful or make large sums of money.

The cost associated with this is incredible but to those who are found guilty and are willing to pay significantly more, these companies will also go through the motions of putting a unit in your car but never actually hooking it up. I was told this happens quite often but once again God supplied me with actual proof of this illegal activity. A few years back while doing some consulting at a company in the area, a female employee had been charged and convicted of driving while intoxicated as she was involved in an accident and fled the scene of her crime. One afternoon shortly after hearing of her conviction I saw the owner of the shop that installed these devices come into the business and meet with upper management. I must admit I was shocked, and I did hide from him as I knew exactly why he was making a house call and it later came out that the unit in her car was not hooked up and she confirmed this to me as she was quite proud of herself. Again, this was not by coincidence that I encountered this and I know God placed me in these many situations so that I may write about it and hope changes can be made. I recently noticed that this particular business is no longer open or listed as a business so maybe the white-collar crime division actually followed up on this since I did inform on this company as well.

CHAPTER 13

THE SUSTAINING

After realizing that I may never be heard let alone vindicated in our court system I decided to stay busy and keep praying for guidance and a resolution and to be honest I didn't fully comprehend how bad this was going to be for me and ended up going through much of my savings between attorney fees, court fees and class fees as well as just living expenses. I continued to look for a job and take small marketing consulting jobs to sustain me. Even though I had twenty years of experience in marketing, operations, and held management level positions for Fortune 500 companies and made six figures as soon as potential employers found out about my record, they would change their mind and tell me they had selected another candidate, and this has not changed even now. I would get through all the interviews with them always moving forward in hiring me but allowing them to do a background check stopped any hope of securing a job. Most companies will not hire an individual with a record not even asking you what it was about. It just isn't done especially with upper management jobs. It was defeating and demoralizing but God heard my prayers and as I tried to stay positive and a few months into the summer I met an older man on the walking trail by my house.

It was quite by chance we started talking and I found out he attended my church as well. I do believe God brings you just the person, the message, and even the circumstance that you need. He told me of a job that delivered medical supplies to patients across the state and some surrounding states. I had nothing to lose, and the company was reputable, and the job seemed admirable, and I always liked to drive and there weren't any other companies wanting to hire me. I don't know if they did a background check, but I would guess not. The court deemed me to be a possible risk while driving while also being a drug felon, two very distinct parts of my job so I can only surmise that God indeed has a sense of humor and had the last laugh and so did I.

The other benefit of this job was the quiet time I had with Jesus, thinking about my life, talking to him, listening and waiting for the next steps. During this time, I was visiting areas of this state that I would have never experienced if it wasn't for this job. It wasn't by chance once again and after mapping it I realized that I had been to virtually every part of this state. I saw all the farms and countryside and the many sunsets realizing how truly beautiful this state is. Experiencing the very wealthy communities as well as the inner city was different in so many ways but alike in that health is the great equalizer and no matter how wealthy you are it cannot buy your life, your parent's life, your spouse's life or very sadly your child's life.

The experience of talking to these patients allowed me to be useful, to pray for them and ask for a healing but I will never know. I do have the satisfaction if nothing else in bringing them their medications offering a smile, a prayer and a genuine concern for them it may have helped. Conducting teaching demonstrations on how to hook up and utilize their feeding tubes was also my job and being fervently patient, which meant a lot when someone is so ill. Often the patients were children, even infants and they and their family needed the support more than anyone. My job became very important to me, and no two days were the same. I thank God for this opportunity as it made me feel useful but also very humble.

I was also volunteering on a regular basis at my church heading up events, negotiating with outside companies, updating databases, and creating what I hoped were operational efficiencies while also helping with the homeless community. My friend Betty Phyllis, who had originally invited me to this church told me that I had met and gotten to know more people in this church in two years than she had in forty years; again, not by chance. My experience in the church spans from January 2012 to present day and in part gave me joy but in part saddened me but also awakened me. I kept a low profile in the church until the Fall of 2013 when I was asked by a new pastor that I had connected with to cohost a Fall Festival for all members and invited guests. One other volunteer position was working with the homeless which I started in 2014 after becoming a member. I must tell you I learned more from them than they did from me. I just listened and gave feedback when they requested it, often overly honest but I was told later by most that they appreciated my honesty. Giving gift cards to homeless people does help them but finding out the reason they are homeless serves them better.

Quite often these souls are addicted to alcohol or drugs and our state over the years has shut many of the state funded facilities causing them to seek shelter elsewhere. Originally funded by the state; Government corruption once again misappropriated funds. Who knows where the money went except in their pockets. The percentage of people in our jail system because of this is mind boggling and even our most recent US States Attorney, after his resignation a few years back stated in a five-page document, that the current number of nonviolent offenders in our jails is wrong on so many levels and they are only in jail because they cannot afford bail or to hire an attorney and the public defender is overburdened. The Sheriff of this county agreed with this and regularly met with nonviolent offenders incarcerated only because they cannot produce bail. It is a sad situation, and everyone agrees, and we can hope for change as they recently passed a bill to reform this. This would release nonviolent offenders but that is not the answer, the answer is reforming the court system and all the players as most of the system remains "pay to play" with the wealthiest getting off instead of their just punishment and the poor getting incarcerated even if not guilty.

I met the previous Governor, in the Fall of 2014 at the train station right before the election. I told him he would win, and he asked me to get involved, vote for him and volunteer. I said I would and within a week after that chance meeting I met our Township committeeman and the mayor of my city at of all places; the church I was attending. Again, coincidence; I know it was not as this journey is not by chance and I have since become my area's precinct captain, an election judge, and was a delegate at the State convention in 2016. I did not volunteer for these positions but was asked to serve so I can only believe God wanted me to experience this and get involved. I got to know the board members of my city and helped get three attorney's elected judge for our county.

I do have a wonderful story about an encounter when I was manning a booth at the Fourth of July festival in my city, and I was with two attorneys' that were running for circuit Judge in their districts. I suggested to them that I would fill the requests and they should concentrate on talking to potential voters. They thought this was a great idea and it was successful but later in the afternoon a thought came to my mind to ask them to respond to a statement near and dear to my heart and they agreed. I stated, "That's just how things are done around here!" I received an immediate reaction from the attorney to my right which was "well that's not right and not in my court room!" The other candidate to my left gave me the status quo answer that every case is different and that's how things work best in the court system. I had received two very clear messages but both obviously so different and I thanked God for showing me this clear distinction between the two candidates. Since being elected, the judge on my right had already been transferred to a larger jurisdiction after only serving for one month at a city court which is virtually unheard of. I expected great things from this man, and he was recently retained for another six years.

I have made it a point when asked to explain my position on the current court system as like a triangle, the lawyers at the bottom, the state's attorneys in the middle and the judges on the top. If you just do the math, it is much easier to monitor the judges and based on the current system of retention; a judge stays on the bench unless they are voted out, but this requires transparency in their court decisions which are not readily available to the public and even when a ruling does make the internet it is taken down in record time. State Senator Lottie Holman O'Neill, a conservative Republican who was the first woman elected to the House of Representatives in 1922 and the first elected to the State Senate in 1950. She wrote, "There is a danger in life tenure of judges using the yes and no ballot, with no opposing candidate. This is the method used by dictators to insure retention in office." A prophetic warning in judicial retention ballots; the answer is yes as only rarely since the blue ballot passed have judges been voted out of office by getting enough no votes.

I will state that an instance of unseating a judge more recently occurred but was orchestrated by the current States Attorney demonstrating her war on corruption, the platform she ran on and some have stated it was race related and this judge was being ousted based on his activity not while a judge but during his time as an Assistant State's Attorney. She was re-elected even though she managed a case that she should have recused herself and stated that she had but decided to go against all legal precedents and absolve a high-profile person from prosecution while also going up against the police chief and even the mayor. When I heard this, I knew God had intervened lending credibility to my story, bringing it into the light and a clear answer to my constant questioning whether to have my story published. I did volunteer for the candidate that opposed her for States Attorney; his message too was to clean up the corruption. He did not win but not too long after the election I came by him again quite by chance at a local retail store. I was in my car parked across from the store when he drove up and dropped off his elderly mother. This encounter was in my town which was at least fifty miles from his neighborhood so again I feel this meeting was meant to be as he instantly recognized me and came over to my car to talk to me. I told him how sorry I was that he didn't win the election for which he thanked me and stated that the people did not get behind him nor did the party. I stated that not many attorneys even his own party would want to change their good thing and support a States Attorney vowing to clean up the corruption in our court system. I told him I could give him information that may help change things if he was interested. He gave me his personal card and I sent him an email but never heard back from him. I'm sure he investigated my case and like the rest of them wanted no part of it, and he thinks it's too political as well, as I have heard countless times.

CHAPTER 14

THE CHURCH – AN UNEXPECTED RESPONSE

My next opportunity to experience the unexpected came in early 2014 after going through the membership training at my church. I kept having this feeling that I needed to share my experience of the corruption with someone, but I hesitated and have found in my experience, when God wants you to do something he will not let it go. I chose to confide in one of the Pastors at the church and he agreed to meet with me and as I started explaining how I came to be at this church starting in January of 2012 he listened but as soon as I started to explain the incident with the cab driver and the police, he proceeded to stop me and explained that his brother was an officer and then proceeded to change the subject entirely and tell me some incredibly sad information concerning one of his children. This did stop me from further explaining what happened to me; honestly, I felt like he was saying buck up girl; like things could be worse so I didn't continue. This was not expected and once again I felt betrayed and now years later his response does make more sense as he may have already known what I went through with his brother-in-law being an officer.

My next attempt in seeking some guidance was from the Senior Pastor and that did not end well either. I wrote to him that it was wonderful visiting with him and his wife and asked him the following question: I know we as Christians forgive the person, but do we forgive the sin especially when it is often accepted behavior but still deemed illegal by our society. Do we turn the other cheek in all cases? I know God will judge all of us, but doesn't God use us for good and change here on earth? Are we not bound to do the right thing? A few days later I received an email that I was accidently copied on stating to another pastor to respond to this question but send it back to her so that she could put it under the Senior Pastor's name as the response.

I was in shock once again and I don't think you get a much clearer message of deception than this, but experiencing this once again caused me to remember what God told me; the lesson is not always and only yours it's often another person's lesson and you are just the instrument in achieving this. We are all sinners, and we all make mistakes, and the lesson wasn't mine, it was and still is theirs. They know who they are and have yet to acknowledge their deception and I have never said anything to anyone as God entrusted me with this information and I believe in his time it will be acknowledged.

So once again I was shut down, but I still felt there was something I needed to do and could not shake the feeling. That feeling stirring in me wouldn't go away and I know that this is the prompting of the Holy Spirit, as it speaks to me and to all of us you just need to listen. If I start tearing up when asking for an answer it signifies to move forward, if I have a feeling of dread then it's telling me to not go there. I take this very seriously now and one should never question the gifts that God has given you. I believe most people just feel it is all coincidence, but I have been right too many times and suffered the consequences of moving ahead when I should have stayed still but also feeling a surge of happiness and well "peace" when I hear and follow his guidance.

After trying to speak to now two pastors at my church without even an acknowledgment I realized that God wanted me to go another path as I didn't believe he had guided me through this maze of corruption for me to remain silent. In the process of becoming a

member a month earlier I met a very kind man who was an Elder
of the church and he was responsible for getting to know us before
we became members and I had found out after reading his bio on
the church site and searching on the internet that he was a retired
Federal agent who headed up many important cases here in this
state. You have to ask with his obvious knowledge of my arrest why
he never asked me anything about it and went ahead and approved
me for membership. I wish he would have asked me before this,
but he eventually was to learn the truth of what I went through
and continued to go through. This was the person God led me to
and I came to trust him without question. I will admit I did put
off talking to him for some time while absorbing all this but when
God wants you to do something he just keeps getting in your head
until you comply. You will have no peace until you do especially if
you are asking to fulfill your purpose. It was not easy, but I knew
it was the right thing to do so I sent him a message asking if he
would meet with me and he agreed, and we decided to meet at the
church. Upon arrival he had a female staff member join us which
I was not aware would be there, but he assured me she would keep
it confidential. She was not very compassionate, making some very
insensitive comments while I relayed the facts, but I believe she did
keep my confidence at least for a while and I also found out that
her son is in the agency as well so this may explain the more recent
activity in regard to investigations. I do believe God orchestrated all
of this for his purpose leading me to Cameron Peters and this was no
coincidence but a little disconcerting as it all seemed too perfect, but
God is like that; only he can make these things happen.

I don't believe he knew what I wanted to talk to him about but
what I do know after hearing the details which of course were not in
any file, and also believing I had suffered a great injustice he wanted
to help me. He was aware of the corruption here in this county and
more specifically in our court system as accepted behavior which I
believe even he did not want to question as I later confirmed. As I
have stated before the corrupt practices work for many as they use it
to their advantage, the attorneys, the prosecutors, the police and the

guilty. It is not coincidence that the corruption in our court system
in this county makes front page news across the country. As I told
him my story, he was empathetic but very professional and I could
tell he was sure he needed to get this information to someone in the
Bureau as he was retired. I don't think anyone really retires from
this organization, but he is very by the book and wouldn't confirm
or deny anything. After our meeting he asked me if I would speak
to someone, I said yes. He said he would be in contact, and he was.
God does have the first and last word in everything.

CHAPTER 15

THE FEDERAL BUREAU OF INVESTIGATION

His first call to me informed me that I would be meeting with agents at the municipal courthouse which I thought was odd since meetings with the Bureau were supposed to be confidential. I was assured of my anonymity as I would not have agreed without this stipulation as I felt my security really was at risk considering the information, I was going to give them and the powerful people it involved. The meeting, originally scheduled for Friday of that week was changed to the following week and the location as it now would be at their offices. I was scheduled to meet with two agents on a Tuesday at 8:30 in the morning. He met me there, introduced me and then left me with two agents; one male agent and a female agent which was also an attorney. I was assured all meetings with the agency were confidential which proved at least in my case to be false, and I was told that talking to anyone about me was a clear violation of their policy to protect all informants. On introductions they were polite and respectful to me but as soon as Cameron left that all changed. The male agent Michael Brian had worked with him years earlier and I felt was either very jealous or resentful of him based on some of his comments to me. I later found out that Cameron worked with Michael Brian's father who was also an agent. Cameron Peters was well known and had attained much attention for bringing to justice a high-level official year earlier while an agent, it was clear they resented him, possibly they didn't want him to once again get credit for uncovering corruption. I am usually right when I feel these things, but I kept it to myself which I probably shouldn't have. I did ask to talk to Cameron after the meeting, but I never brought this up to him, I wish I had but this was all new territory for me and to be honest after my meeting with them I was apprehensive to say anything.

Based on their initial questions I believed they had already been in contact with at least the States Attorney's office if not others as they knew some of the details of my case that only those that were involved would have known which is so very wrong since they were the ones that should have been under investigation. As I stated the meeting was contentious at best and I felt I was on trial all over again. Being interviewed for almost three hours ... I must have been telling them something they felt important, or they would have ended the meeting/interrogation. I felt at the time their initial meeting with the States Attorney's office was not complete, only hearing of what had transpired in the last year apparently knowing nothing of what had transpired before as they seemed unaware of the Unlawful Restraint cab incident. They were also unaware of the corrupt high-level company I worked for that fired me the day after I received the expungement approval or that I was arrested five days later and the very day I spoke to the State Police about the expungement. They were only told what the attorney's wanted them to know, and I was soon to learn how powerful Larry George truly was and was told no one would have gone up against him; apparently that included the Bureau. I expected better of them, always believing they were the premier law enforcement that was not corruptible which in recent years has proven to the contrary. It became clear that they weren't going to help me, but they didn't mind taking information that would help them in other areas. I was expendable.

I had no reason to lie as I achieved nothing by talking to them, there were no deals and all it proceeded to do is further bury my chances to be heard and get any justice in my case. They did know who Larry George was and asked how I came to hire him. I told them I was referred to him by an acquaintance and they seemed to believe me. He did state that the 402 conferences are legal even though he agreed they seem suspect. Suspect? Having your attorney, the prosecutor and the judge going into a conference to discuss the case without you present? When I told the two agents about the company I worked for and their apparent corruption they were very interested, and I am sure they utilized this information benefitting them and taking credit for anything they uncovered. When I relayed my story about a certain County Sheriff trying to get to know me on the train and trying to date me, he listened but then blew it off that he was probably just interested in me. Also, County sheriffs do not ride the train while on duty and in uniform, at least that is what I have been told. When I brought up the three high powered nails flattening my tire after I left the monitoring device systems shop, he seemed interested and listened but did not question me on it further, but I believe he didn't want to give me any reason to believe there was anything incorrect or illegal that had transpired. This, I believe is their way. They collect information and neither confirm nor deny.

So as a tactic they instill doubt, creating fear so that you remain silent and this is the investigation they performed, not delving into the courts and the attorney's illegal practices but utilizing really anything that would prove to unnerve me. Once again, I experienced intimidation but now from what I thought were also the "good guys." They intimidate and demean; they thanked me especially for the information on the company I worked for and told me don't call us we we'll call you. Talking to the bureau just put a target on my back opening my case up to all state employees, prosecutors, judges and attorneys and it is still uncertain the system will ever right this wrong just because I did the right thing. They should not wonder why people do not come forward if they are not going to be protected. I do not for the record, believe Cameron Peters would have expected this would happen to me and I knew he believed me and also believed I had nothing to worry about in speaking to them, but it mattered little as after a few hours of hearing the facts they proceeded to tell me that nothing the court or my attorneys did was illegal.

That same day after the meeting I sent an email to Cameron asking to speak to him and he immediately replied that there was no planned investigation. So, it was confirmed and as I stated I believed they had already spoken to someone at the States Attorney's office the previous Friday and they interviewed me to be thorough or just check it off but never intended to do anything against these attorneys and government officials. If I had gotten some confirmation from them that indeed there was illegal activity which there was, and they were going to investigate then I could have had some recourse against the injustice I experienced.

It would not have been inappropriate to at least direct me to an attorney that could have helped me, but they did not. There is no confirmation our meeting even existed as there is no record on file. I did see, although only for a few minutes the bureau file on me at the courthouse as this was handed to me as my file by mistake by a clerk but was retrieved out of my hands within minutes by the Supervisor. When I questioned him, he told me it was not my file and walked away. So much for our right to know information that directly involves you and frightening to realize how our rights no longer exist. I believed the FBI is and was supposed to be the bottom-line decision makers based on recommendations but as we have seen in recent days that may not be true. I am only reporting on the facts as I have lived through it. It is not surprising that so much now is coming to light on the behavior of the Bureau but as you an see this is not new as this transpired in 2014. If the highest levels at the Bureau, the DOJ and others assume they do not have to follow the law then it does not surprise me that they feel they are untouchable and proceed as they choose. The Bureau should not be swayed by any official no matter who he or she is and how powerful their positions. With the firing of the Director of the FBI in past years and the most recent corruption exposed in the last two years I see this as a clear direction of where we are headed. This is again not by chance and I'm sure my story is one of many yet to come out and when exposed at such high levels it allows more opportunity to hear from others as they may not feel so alone in their trials.

CHAPTER 16

INSINUATES INTO LIFE ONCE AGAIN

Within days after my conversation with the agents I was confronted at the gym by Mike Joseph, the same man who had given me attorney Rich Steven's contact information a year earlier and would continue over the years to insinuate himself into my case and my privacy. He asked me how he handled my case which was interesting because I never confirmed to him that I had even called him let alone hired him. He then proceeded to tell me he heard there was an investigation at the courthouse and asked me if I knew anything about it to which I replied that I knew nothing about it. This information had to come to him from Rich Stevens and so much for maintaining attorney -client privilege. He has little consideration for his oath and the States Attorney handling the information in my case had little consideration for my safety that is apparent. Even with them stating there was no investigation into my case I did uncover the following that would directly contradict this:

The original prosecutor on my case, Clark Michaels currently has no history of ever working as a state's attorney in this state. There are some stories concerning cases still on the internet, which is most likely him, but they appear only up until the summer of 2014, a month after telling my story to the FBI. Many of the transcripts in my court appearances no longer have his name listed but have been changed to Prosecutor only but I do have copies of the originals. He currently is living in another state, which from what I can determine was where he was originally from, no longer a prosecutor but a practicing attorney just like his father who also resides there. I looked him up on LinkedIn shortly after I told my story and just know when one looks a person up on LinkedIn that person does become aware of who is looking at their profile. There is a private mode but not using it allowed him to view my picture, realize who I was and prompted him to do something that confirmed his guilt. After realizing I was viewing his profile, he proceeded to change his name on his profile from Clark Michael to Clark M. (again not his real name). Now the question comes to mind, if you have nothing to hide well why the deception? I would suspect that he lost his license in this state but retained his license in his home state. I would also gather since they allowed him to do this that he agreed not to testify against those involved and quietly left.

Another change that occurred after speaking to the Bureau, and within a week was that my female probation officer was replaced and they assigned a new probation officer to me and when I proceeded to look this man up on LinkedIn I found two profiles for him; one stating he had recently become a probation officer here in this state with little information but also another profile stating that he was a retired government official heading up the probation division in the same state which is home to the FBI, that being Virginia. There was no picture available, but I later confirmed years later it was him when he did place a picture with his profile. When we first met, he asked me about the case which I found odd, but I told him I was not guilty and explained it all once again. He listened intently and then stated that I did not have to come back in, but I could just send in the documents with my payment. It was obvious they didn't want me around, but they also did not want to concede any wrongdoing and just wanted to contain it. I do believe he was transferred here based on the Bureau recommendation and brought out of retirement to monitor the situation and well, me.

Within a few weeks of my speaking to the FBI, there were incidences that were not mere coincidences although they would want you to believe this. I heard from my friend and colleague, the former human resource manager at CB Account. She had recently moved to Arizona and had been working part time as a consultant for the cosmetic company she had worked at for years and she emailed me that she was abruptly fired from this company with no reason given. I didn't know what to say to her as the FBI told me to not speak to anyone about what we discussed. I can only suspect her name came up when the FBI started the investigated and also investigated the previous company, we both worked for; CB Account. I will concede the information could have been leaked inside the states attorney's office and disseminated to the various attorneys involved and we need to remember the Vice President of CB Account was and still is an active attorney. This would not surprise me as I stated, my file at the courthouse was an open book for any attorney to view and they all think nothing of discussing your case with all who are interested. Client confidentiality: this doesn't exist and there is no privacy.

Two weeks after meeting with the FBI there was an incident concerning this states Senator's son as he was arrested and charged in another state with aggravated assault of a woman. The news article stated that he had groped a woman at a bar, was arrested but it was "unclear whether he had an attorney representing him" in court as no one showed up and he was subsequently released. I can only assume that the FBI was trying to confirm that Larry George was indeed the Senator's private attorney and possibly catch him doing something illegal in another state. It seems the limitless power and manipulation even crosses state lines as they are the FBI and I believe they should be able to do their jobs in the most effective means but at what cost and for all we know this woman he assaulted could have been a plant, setting him up to ensure an arrest as it all seemed very contrived and within weeks of my talking to them.

Shortly after Cameron Peters agreed to help me as he could see that the authorities were not going to do anything for me and in actuality terminating any chance of the actual facts of my case getting heard. He responded asking me to send him the facts of the case which I did and after his review he sent me a message stating that he had read my fact statement and that he had forwarded to a friend for his review and recommended action. He also stated that he was sorry that I had to go through this injustice but that it is helpful to remember that all things work for his glory even in difficult situations where we are the clear victim.

I knew at this point he had investigated all the facts of my case, found them to be true and agreed with me that the FBI knew the truth and still I was expendable. This email that I retained for my records was deleted from my email in 2019 but I knew to keep a copy as it was the truth, and I was relieved that he believed me. The man he forwarded my statement to, who was a very high-powered attorney spoke to me but in the end stated that my case was too political and refused to represent me. This has not changed over the years as it takes a very brave person to do the right thing in this world.

CHAPTER 17

THE MANY ROADBLOCKS

In 2015 I secured a job at a major corporation requiring me to obtain a state PERC card (permanent employee registration card) to do my job. This was not a great job, but I needed it as no one else would hire me. I was denied my PERC card initially based on the existing record on me and was requested to attend a hearing where I would go before a board and discuss my background. They asked me to explain my situation and as I explained the details of my case, not holding anything back and as a closing statement I informed them that I did not buy verdicts. They all looked at each other, smiled and then granted permission. This would not have happened if they were not aware of the facts of my case and for the record, Judge Thomas retired from the bench two weeks later.

During this time which would have been the Fall of 2015, I decided to try to once again get my case expunged or at least sealed as I was having little success at getting any attorney to take up my cause. I spoke to three attorneys in one month that were more than happy to represent me and quote me their fee even after mentioning the possible statute or timeframe, but it was only after they checked my file at the courthouse and found out the details of my case, who represented me and that I had spoken to the FBI that they failed to return my calls. Many attorneys' take expungement cases that on paper state a statutory timeframe must be met before requesting a sealing or expungement, but this statute also states that it is up to the judge to determine the outcome. As I have found it is up to a certain States Attorney to hear why it should be expunged, not based on anything but a fabulous fee as an inducement. If you are trying to seek justice, then don't bother as the Supervisor States Attorney and as well a certain Judge stated in two separate conversations with me that it's not their duty to retry cases. I would say true on paper, but it is a fine line as they all have taken an oath to seek justice in all cases. If you have the right attorney anything is possible, remember Rich Stevens told me we would just keep going before the Judge until they say yes. It is the Judge that will give a final ruling in court taking the prompting of the state's attorney handling the case to set aside the verdict but only for a fee. The Judge seldom knows the facts as the decision of yea or née and the amount of money to change hands has already been agreed to before they get to court. So, the recent activity of the States Attorney letting a certain high-profile person skate is not uncommon as I am sure there was a high dollar agreement as an inducement to make it happen not just the bond amount that has been suggested.

After months of trying, I did find an attorney willing to at least meet with me, we will call her Patty Lynn and she too had been a former prosecutor and was willing to listen. As I was relaying my information, she was sympathetic and promptly said no problem and took a check from me for a thousand dollars. Her being a former States Attorney she would have known about the statute but said nothing about it in our meeting. She did tell me some stories and informed me that Larry George had been given anger management classes due to his outbursts in court and assault on a certain prosecutor. She also told me of Judge Thomas making fun of her when she was nine months pregnant with twins. She had seen it all and shared this with me for a reason, again no coincidence that this woman even being a prior states attorney was not respected.

As I stated it didn't take her long to find out who I was and back off from the case right before my court date. She did say there was no affidavit in my file and that she did not talk to Rich Stevens about my case, but I believe she did as they are all incestuous, covering for each other and I'm sure they both agreed that I was not guilty, but it just wasn't worth their careers to chance representing me. I did find the affidavit a month later in my file of which she stated in an email was not there, no doubt placed there by Rich Stevens, covering his tracks at her prompting. I know she believed me, but again, it wasn't worth it to her to go out on a limb and affect her career. She did the paperwork for me and told me to give it to the judge as she would not represent me in court. She also stated that she thought I had been through a lot and after the hearing she would be happy to show me how to fill out the paperwork to file a complaint against my previous attorneys with the American Bar Association. Taking out three of the most successful attorneys on the take certainly wouldn't hurt her and would only help her career. She is now in private practice and a professed Christian at least on social media. I wondered what God put on her heart about her lack of doing the right thing in my case after all the lesson is hers and she will either learn it now or later, but I assure you it will come around again they always do especially to self-professed Christians who ask God to guide them. I found out a year later she was let go from her previous prestigious law firm headed up by a retired judge shortly after taking my case and failing to represent me. God does fulfill his promises to refine and guide.

Almost a year later in April of 2016, I once again applied for sealing but did not have time to hire an attorney as my sister had recently passed away from a sudden heart attack in June. I was very sad, actually devastated but I did go to court in August just to see if this time they would hear me as they did have the facts of the case and maybe she would do the right thing this time. Since I was representing myself which is called prose; the paperwork comes directly to you so the States Attorney could not discredit it as I had these document in my possession. The reports indicated that they agreed to granting the sealing of my case so I was hopeful the public shaming would be over and maybe get back my career, but it mattered little.

When I appeared before Judge Williams he immediately once again denied my request but did allow me to speak. As I was relaying what I had gone through and the facts of the case he stopped me. The prosecutor remained silent which again was odd, but I feel he knew I was going to be there and was only told to deny my petition. Once I obtained the transcript of my court appearance, I found it had been altered with the court saying so much more and my words being altered and actually deleted. They knew the local police and state police had granted the sealing of the records with only the states attorney denying me and subsequent denial of my application by the judge but still a month later after once again looking at my physical file at the courthouse I now found an official letter from the local police records clerk personally addressed to the judge denying that they had approved the sealing. I did not see such a letter coming from the State Police as I don't believe they can be swayed to do such a thing. The benefit: yes, there is one, is that sitting through the many cases as I was scheduled to appear last in both court appearances did serve a purpose as I was forced to sit and listen to the many cases and their outcomes. Being scheduled last was not a coincidence but was an assurance that others and especially attorneys were not going to hear about my case. I sat through case after case with them getting their expungement granted even though many did not meet the statutory time limit with a few even having additional charges against them. Granting their petitions was the presiding Judge Michael William's responsibility but filtered through the Assistant State's Attorney. Those that were granted their wish all had attorneys with them and it was apparent they had secured the outcome ahead of time. One woman going before the court without an attorney, who obviously did not know the rules, had applied for expungement of a twenty-year-old DUI and failed even though she had no further incidences and no additional charges since this time. She was a teacher and she told them she would not be able to secure a job promotion in her district with this on her record. This didn't seem to matter to either the states attorney or the judge.

CHAPTER 18

THE YEARS
CONTINUED

Over the next three years I checked my file at the courthouse many times only to either find a supposed missing document miraculously added or as far as the transcripts, altered. I found the motion to quash which was never filed in the court by Larry George or Rich Stevens but in my file months later with my signature forged. I found the request to withdraw my plea addressed to Judge Thomas instead of the supposed request of another Judge. I found the affidavit that wasn't there miraculously appear. In relation to the altered court room transcripts in my case, which it took quite a bit of time to receive after requesting them but I did also have the original transcripts.

Just as I thought I would finish my story and this was in 2017, yes with little achieved justice but a greater understanding of his ways and send it to the publishers God gave me the opportunity to once again experience our court system. There was a glimmer of hope that those who had gone down the wrong path would turn and do the right thing but that opportunity, even handed to them on a silver platter did not shake them and they reverted to their illegal behavior, lying, covering up and diverting attention. Staying in contact with those men that were still interested in justice and after supplying them additional facts concerning my ongoing case and with Larry George now gone from this earth; dying from an apparent heart attack in the Fall of 2016 they may have seen a way to move forward allowing this injustice to be finally turned around. Allowing this man although powerful to dictate to the authorities what would be considered and condoned would only continue for so long, God is the higher authority and will have the last word and this was and is without question.

After receiving all details of what I went through my friend informed me that the Assistant State's Attorney was open to the expungement of my case and that the presiding judge was soon to retire, and this would be the time to get this accomplished. Now please know this is done all the time regardless of the statutory time limits for a 1410 probation, which by the way is not a conviction. Before this court date I was told by my contact that Ms. Lorna had contacted my previous attorney Rich Stevens to inform him that she was willing to expunge my case. She did this without first speaking to me and I was told he had agreed to represent me and was told the date and time to show up and although I found this incredible and had little faith this was going to have a good outcome; I was willing to give him the opportunity to finally do the right thing. Apparently, he did agree to represent me when talking to Anne Lorna, not remembering my name but after Satan himself reminding him of who he was and continues to be he changed his mind and then questioned her on the legality of it. When I was asked to contact him concerning representing me I did tell him of my hesitation but also stated that if he were willing to turn around and do the right thing in representing me I would not be opposed to talking to him. I left a message for him, and he did call me back but as soon as I heard his voice a level of anxiety rose in me, and I knew in my heart he would not do right thing. His first question to me was who I knew for this to happen, responding to his question and not knowing really what to say I told him I knew many people. Not getting anywhere he went on giving me his legal talk about what the law states concerning 1410 probation. I proceeded to tell him I had heard many cases while sitting through two days of cases a year ago that all were granted, and it was up to the Judge and his discretion. I also reminded him of

PERFECTED FOR THE PURPOSE

what he told me when he represented me, on how things are done. He didn't like this but was cautious as usual and I knew right then and there this would not end well.

He said he didn't know how we could get my case expunged legally but that he would talk to another judge about my getting my case reversed meaning there were errors in how my case was handled, and he would get back to me. Errors, no they were more than errors and he was just as accountable. I was glad he admitted this but felt this still would not happen. I went to court on the day I was originally told to be there by the State's Attorney as this is what I felt God was telling me to do and I was hoping I could represent myself prose. He did not show up in court but an officer of the court who knew my circumstances made a call to him and told him I was there. He proceeded to tell him that he was at another court hearing on another case which I immediately felt was a lie but later I was told by the officer that he would be at the courthouse around 1:45 to meet him there. I decided to sit and wait to talk to the States Attorney which I did after almost two hours of hearing cases. When confronted she said that Rich Stevens never called her back, so I was not on the docket to be heard and it was clear she wanted nothing to do with me. I also knew this was a lie as I was positive, they had spoken about my case and how they should avoid it. She did however say that I could go through her directly which again doesn't surprise me as I believe they all work this way, but it was the presiding Judge's last day and in reality, she could have allowed me to go before him but she had not secured her fee up front so it would not happen.

I was once again saddened by the corruption but not surprised. As I left the courthouse once again in defeat and heading for my car I was prompted to speak to a woman in the elevator; not really knowing why but not questioning my feeling. I asked her how her day was, and she proceeded to tell me her attorney didn't show up but called her telling her to still go to court and check in and he would reschedule her court date and talk to her later. I asked her who her attorney was and no surprise it was Rich Stevens. It was clear he did not want to be anywhere near me that day, the States Attorney or the circumstance he was placed in, he would not be boxed in, and I informed my contacts of this. How clever of him but it just made his guilt more apparent to those watching and especially the gentlemen I was working with to get this injustice resolved. After this encounter I decided to call him and push him for an explanation and he stated he would be in room 110 representing another client requesting a 402 conference with that presiding judge and told me he would ask him about me during this conference which I feel he never did but he wanted me to believe he was helping me. After an hour he called me and responded that the judge would need to make sure nothing would come back to him and I would have to sign an agreement to never speak about it or write about it and he would agree to vacate my sentence. Now once again I would never even consider doing this and I believe he knew this and I know he never even spoke to this judge but wanted to see if I would first agree to his terms. I also felt he may be trying to set me up. First of all, if this could truly be done then why have I had to wait so long with so many attorneys and judges and federal employees knowing what happened to me? So, I did not agree to his terms and in retaliation and to cover himself he told Anne Lorna that Judge Marc had denied my request I of course informed her I never went before him so that could not even be possible.

I believe my sentence should be vacated and those responsible should be held accountable for their actions. Making enemies in this county is dangerous especially if you are trying to do the right thing but God is my refuge and he will guide me as he always has. As I waited for my contacts to get back to me I once again came across news that will only further the corruption in this court. It seems that Judge Jill has been named the presiding judge and to remind you she is the judge that first heard my case in 2013 with Larry George representing me and we came before her not just once by twice. She was the daughter of his law partner; which legally should have prompted her to recues herself from my case of which she did not. Also, she advanced my case to go to trial without a motion to quash being presented on my behalf which if she had heard the motion to quash she would have had to dismiss the case against me. This woman in this municipal court, with her in this position and her young age secures how things will be done now and going forward for the next twenty years.

In the Fall of 2017, I was instructed to contact the States Attorney and ask for her help which she herself stated I could contact her directly. I did this once again knowing this would not go well, which it didn't. She stated Rich Stevens had contacted her and told her that Judge Marc had ruled not to vacate my sentence. I told her I had never been in front of Judge Marc which prompted her question who did I go in front of which I told her that I had not been in front of a Judge since my expungement hearing in 2016 and before that in 2013. She replied Judge Marc was taking the cases of Thomas and I told her once again I never appeared in front of Judge Marc and that Rich Stevens never acted on my behalf. I asked her again what had changed in righting this obvious injustice that she was willing to take care of a few month earlier. She at that point stated she never agreed and hung up on me. I hope she is thinking about her job and that as a public servant she took an oath to always seek the truth in all cases, right a wrong and seek justice even though having the title of prosecutor. I do believe prosecutors need to be reminded of this and not just win every case even at the cost of someone's reputation. I am sure she is well aware of the FBI investigation as her name appeared on my FBI file located at the courthouse where she resides. Once again covering for one another, it is an incestuous group that is a fact.

CHAPTER 19

WHERE MY CASE STAYS

As I stated my last court appearance at this point, attempting an expungement was in the summer of 2016 and since I represented myself the paperwork came to my attention, so I did notice that I was eligible for expungement in February 2018. I wanted to represent myself which I should have but once again I was prompted by my source get an attorney; this time he provided the name of three attorneys that he stated, "knew the system." I selected one of the three and he was a previous states attorney as were the rest of them and I assumed he was honest since he was recommended by my friend. I must say that meeting with Stan Michaels for the first time was a good experience as he listened to me, took notes and told me without question he could help me. The request was filed in February and was not scheduled to go before a judge until June as he stated to me, he was waiting for Judge Grimes and not the presiding Judge Jill. This made sense to me for the time delay, and I was told I did not need to appear which I found very odd but did not question it as I really didn't relish going into another court room.

I did have a thought on why my presence was not requested is that I recently and early in the year had an encounter the presiding judge as well as other judges when a woman's group that I was a board member on had toured the courthouse and after had lunch with them. It was only supposed to be the one judge who helped us set up the tour joining us for lunch but seems word got around and not one, but five judges showed up. In any case I found it incredible that I wound up sitting directly across from the very judge that could have helped me obtain justice years earlier following the law but instead acted on her own and her father's partner's best interests; yes, I was sitting across from Judge Jill herself. She did not remember me, but I am told she thought I was quite knowledgeable on the current issues and I was also sitting across from Judge Marc who per Rich Stevens had denied vacating my sentence a few months earlier; he didn't know me either, surprised? What I do know is that news of this meeting did scare the Supervisor State's Attorney who also attended, stating to me quite out of the blue once again that it is not up to the States Attorney's Office to retry cases. I did not plan this meeting to happen but it is clear to me as it should be to you that only God could make this encounter possible, to be sitting directly across from the very face of corruption.

After waiting for months, my attorney Stan Michaels represented me on a Friday and he called me shortly after stating that the case was sealed only and not expunged. He stated he requested the expungement as was requested in the paperwork but it was denied. I did not believe him and proceeded to go to the court house a few days later requesting my file only to be told after waiting an hour that it did not exist which I was informed meant it was expunged. While I was waiting at one point a county police officer showed up and spoke to the person helping me at the court house. He kept looking over at me and finally came over to talk to me and took my name and said he would call me, I never heard from him.

I left but headed downstairs to request the transcript of my case. I received it a few days later and did find that Stan Michaels did go before Judge Jill and not Judge Grimes, and he didn't ask for an expungement in my case and actually stated to Judge Jill that he made a mistake in the paperwork and was only requesting the sealing of my case. This is all in the transcripts and he thought I would never find out what he did and of course he would never return my calls. I did receive an email from the arresting Police Department Administrator ninety days later that my case was sealed, not expunged but only sealed. Not feeling entirely sure of it even being sealed I requested a FOIA report via email in March of 2019, seven months after it was supposedly sealed. They did not even verify who I was in this correspondence so anyone could have requested this information under my name and what I received was the full report and obviously not sealed. I sent the email to Stan Michaels and he immediately responded, something he had not done in the last eight months since my court date. He got them to redact certain information and then started avoiding me once again.

I did continue contacting him to discuss it but he would not return my calls and at one point I decided to drive to his office but upon arrival I was told by his assistant that he was not there. As I sat outside his office contemplating what I would do now, within minutes he emerged and was picked up by another car parked on the street. I did feel he was tipped off that I was near his office and he prepared to avoid me. Continuing to have the feeling there was something still not right regarding the sealing of my case, my missing file at the courthouse and the people who were covering, once again God was telling me there was yet more to come.

CHAPTER 20

MY CHURCH

Outside of my case and the disruption and distress it caused me over the years, my own church added to this in several ways. I believe Cameron Peters and others kept my case a secret but really why would they want this information and the many illegal acts public knowledge? I didn't tell anyone else and in 2016 after serving on the security team for two years I was asked to step down by the leader of the group due to my forwarding a message about a registered sex offender that was in the church. On a certain Sunday in September this man had gone downstairs amongst the children's Sunday school classes. It seems this man was a member of the church but had been arrested while in another state on business by soliciting a young girl online and the local police arrested him when he went to meet this young girl in an undercover sting. I did not judge this man but only escalated it to the leadership and in return my history was now to be exposed. It seems a certain person on the security team felt it the appropriate time to tell all he knew about my case and of course, he only shared what the police report stated. He knew nothing of the cab incident or the facts leading up to it and it is possible he felt I deserved it since I exposed this man for his offenses. In any case the gossip was rampant and still is today although I believe much truth has come out since this time.

In September of 2018 I had received a member email from my church that a wonderful young man that I knew and who had worked for the church had passed away. Since there were no details given and I was Facebook friends with him, I looked him up but with no mention of his passing I did write a brief message. Well, this action prompted a whole new series of actions; including an employee from the church showing up at the gym to talk to me. He never acknowledged that he was sent but I had never seen him there before and I would never see him there again. He was a nice man as I worked with him on several volunteer activities and I was relieved to see him as I was hoping he could shed some light about his passing. I was not prepared for what he was about to tell me, that he had thrown himself in front of a train, taking his own life. He told me that he suffered from a Bipolar disorder and that it was deemed a suicide and that at the time of his death he was once again working at the church of which I was not aware of as I believed he was still attending school in Florida. I was very sad and did attend his service at the church that following Saturday and as I sat in the back within minutes a pastor came up and sat next to me. He asked several questions about how I knew him, when I saw him last and he then started asking me what kind of car I had and it became obvious he was put up to this; looking for information somehow attaching me to what happened. It was the local police I am certain that put him up to this based on my still in existence record and also based on the 2016 sex offender issue that local police were aware of. What I did conclude is this young man had taken his own life while working at the very church that had judged me and maligned me and well; he died on their watch; that is what I know.

It was at this time I believe the local Police Department who were regularly employed by this church had started monitoring my calls; assuming I was a person of interest but they of course never reached out to me even though I knew many of them and for the record it had to be very easy to determine that I was never in contact with this young man just by phone records alone and of course the lack of Facebook messages between us. This did not stop the monitoring as it gave them the now legal opportunity to investigate me, my case and all the corruption surrounding it let alone my talking to the FBI. They also proceeded to inquire about both my sister's death and my mother's death talking to the neighbors trying to link me to something; anything I believe. I decided to send a letter to Cameron Peters, who I had not spoken to since February of 2018. I wasn't going to bother him, but I did feel he needed to know once again what had transpired in my case, with this attorney, and once again in this corrupt court system and I also wanted him to know about the police investigation and the monitoring of my calls and see if he could offer any assistance. He received my letter on a Saturday, sent me an email stating he received it and that he could talk to me the following week. This was not unlike him as I know he always gave himself enough time to investigate everything we were to discuss before talking to me. I did send this letter to his home as I didn't trust they were not monitoring my emails and it was actually to his benefit respecting his privacy, but he didn't seem to see it that way. The night he called me the first words he stated was "I'm married" my reply was "yes, I know Mary" which is his wife. I had known this man for four years and it was never anything but professional based on my case and he knew this. He may have been upset at the content of my letter but what I wrote was only factual and I thought information he should know. Since this was December of 2018 and I had not yet found out my file had not been sealed which I would not find out until March of 2019; the conversation was decidedly short, stating to me that the outcome of my case under Stan Michaels was fine and as well he stated the Police have every right to monitor my calls. I would agree if they indeed had a warrant to do this which I am sure they did not and after all warrants need to be renewed every thirty days based on their findings. I was shocked by his response and saddened; I wrapped up the call very quickly knowing he had no further intention of helping me. Shortly after this my email account was hacked and all the emails concerning my involvement with the security team at the church were removed. The correspondence from Cameron Peters confirming not only the facts of my case but also stating I was the clear victim was also deleted. Yes, they did delete them from my account but were still on my iPhone and for the record I do have all of them and as well I have the IP addresses and corresponding home addresses of those that infiltrated my system. Eventually this software that helped me determine this information was blocked from my use and only high-level authorities can make this happen. The monitoring of my calls continued although as I stated, I don't believe there was an active warrant for this to happen and since warrants to monitor calls legally have to be renewed monthly based on solid information of a crime; I didn't see it possible. In other words, they needed to prove I was a threat. The only threat I posed and still today is exposing the truth.

CHAPTER 21

MONITORING AND TRACKING

This is where my case has been left as every time I tried in the past and continue today to contact an attorney, someone contacts them to not take my case and as well it seemed the local police department was always notified. In May of 2019, not wanting to use my phone, giving them access to my every move and conversation, I decided to contact my next potential attorney by physically stopping by his office on a Thursday to make an appointment for the following Saturday. I got to his area earlier than my appointment time and I made the mistake of calling his office to inform them that I could come in earlier if they wanted me to, leaving a message with the receptionist. She called me back within minutes and told me to come in. When I got to his office there were two police vehicles parked outside of his office. I thought this was odd but went in not realizing this was the start of the continued intimidation by various law enforcement agencies now not just in my own city or surrounding areas but in every city depending on where I was.

When I met with this new attorney, who by the way had a reputation of doing the right thing he seemed a little short with me but told me to tell him about my case. I believe they were recording the call or at least listening in which again is illegal in this two-party consent state. After hearing my story, he asked me how I got his information, and I informed him I met a friend of his and she referred him to me. By the look on his face, he knew who I was talking about and I believe she told him at least part of my story as he too had experienced corruption within the FBI when running for a local office. He handed me his card and asked if there was something else, I wanted to tell him. This prompted me to believe he had heard from someone other than my last attorney who not only has many connections in the legal community but in law enforcement as he was not only a States Attorney but a Chief of Police for this county. This explained why the officers were outside his office. I left without telling him of the monitoring and the issues with the church and I kept thinking of why he asked me if I wanted to tell him something more so I did email him later asking him if someone had contacted him and he confirmed but would not indicate who it was. I believe it was someone on behalf of the church but for the record I had no intention of talking to an attorney about the church incident although I should have and maybe this harassment would have ended instead of it continuing today in 2023.

In June I decided to contact a company to at least help me identify who was listening in on my calls as it didn't look promising to retain any attorney until I could accomplish this. A retired FBI agent was the co-owner of this company and I had been referred to before on another matter and his partner was also connected and an attorney. I stopped by on a Friday and got an appointment for Monday, once again not using my phone. I left my phone at home the day of the meeting just to be sure I was not tracked but at the last minute, being apprehensive, realizing that no one knew where I was, I sent an email from my other phone to a friend giving him information where I was and who I was going to meet and that I would call him when I was done.

I went into the office and was greeted by Christopher Keith, the attorney which surprised me because I thought I was meeting with Bill Daniels, the retired FBI agent. We sat down and I began once again explaining my situation hoping he would help me but within a few minutes he received a call on his cell phone, which he answered which I thought was odd while in a meeting with a new client. He looked at me while he listened to this caller, a sure sign it had something to do with me and then agreed and hung up. He apologized and continued to hear my story and in closing he said he would be in touch. The next day, as agreed I sent him an email along with my phone records clearly showing my calls were being monitored. He responded a few days later after I again emailed him, stating he was going to follow through on our discussion. This of course never happened; he didn't help me; in contrast I now became the investigated once again and as well; the monitored. I stopped by his office a month later to follow up with him and instead met his receptionist who stated he was in his office and on the phone, which wasn't true as I heard a noise behind me since I had left the entrance door opened. I saw him go out a door down the hall slipping into another room and it was obvious to me at that point that he utilized a back entrance to avoid me, how clever. I told her that I just saw him leave and she seemed a little upset and stated that he was going on vacation, didn't have time to meet with me and that she would give him the message to call me. I left knowing I would never hear from him and I thought it best as no one knew I was there. I didn't try again but since this time it was stated on the internet shortly after they had moved their offices to a new location and that Bill Daniels, the retired FBI Agent had changed his profile, no longer part of this company that he cofounded but now his own company. Most recently this being 2021 on the internet they are listed as still partners and for the record they are still at the same office as I visited. They also state they have offices in another city with Bill Daniel now as an attorney. But for the record there is no such attorney practicing in this state.

Christopher Keith; the man I initially met with and a founding partner was the Chief of the High-Tech crimes Bureau in this state previous to starting this company and who is still registered and active as an attorney in this state although recently it has changed from active in 2019 and as well in 2020 up to 2021 to not active today. I believe he feels this absolves him of his legal obligation to me after hearing my case; instead becoming employed by the very people who were invading my privacy; the very reason I contacted him. Over the next month I contacted four other attorneys to take my case with not one responding to my calls which is very odd for any attorney not to at least hear from the potential client; unless of course someone has asked them not to. This pattern of not returning my calls continued for some time but eventually this changed since I put a note about this behavior on my phone and I believe potential attorneys were then instructed meet with me, to hear me out and then just refuse the case. Yes, this worked for them but there is always that one or two who you can count on to have a conscience and at least confirm your suspicions.

In June moving forward with other activities and my political group; I asked the police to present at our meeting on the topic of privacy and internet security. I was going to contact the community officer that had last presented to our group but since our meeting place was in a different city I was told to contact the Community Officer there. No one called me back so I emailed them getting a response from an officer stating they did not do those types of meetings. This is when I noticed my Gmail was once again compromised but now by this local Police department and I do once again have the IP address to confirm this. It then became apparent to me that one of my friends knew this officer as I saw him on her Facebook contacts. I hadn't seen her in many years but she did show up at a certain chiropractor's office at the same time I was there and asked many detailed questions about both my sister's passing and as well, my mother's passing. I answered her questions but let's just say that law enforcement really should not use these informants to do their work as they usually are not very good at it, but it does I guess allow them to get answers when they have not obtained the legal authority to do so. In mid-July I did capture another IP address that had logged into my computer and after running a trace on this address, I determined it had come from an attorney that was a member of my church and this did not surprise me as I believe they could use him so that all costs for enlisting the more recent Private Investigators would be hidden at least temporarily.

Select Meetings and Invasive Practices

Throughout the rest of the summer and into the Fall I was contacted by various people to "talk," most being from the church. I was contacted by the woman that originally told me about the sex offender in the church. She asked me to meet her for dinner after almost two years of not hearing from her. It didn't take long for it to become obvious she was recording our conversation as I saw a gray strap on her shoulder that obviously had lost its adhesion and that she kept playing with. I confirmed she had to have spoken to someone at the church that put her up to this and when I mentioned that I had screen shots of all of the conversations, she stated "oh the screen shots" and this was all I needed to confirm she was put up to this and I decided to not confront her then but I did later in the Fall. It was quite disconcerting that the woman that had started all of this with the church by telling me of the sex offender would betray me, but that is exactly what happened. She knew what she did in escalating the information on the sex offender was the right thing to do but she wasn't willing to stand up now for me I have not heard from her since and she also deleted me as a friend on Facebook. I also met with a man at his request; also, from the church who I ushered with previously in the church. When I got to the restaurant I realized that right across the street was the office building that housed a branch office of the FBI and the exact place where they interrogated me for almost three hours! Once at the table he proceeded to put a recording device on the table meant to look like his phone and proceeded to ask me many questions. I also was informed that the son of a church member and an FBI agent may have been part of this, and I knew of her son previous to this meeting because she had told me of him in my original meeting with Cameron Peters.

Later in September my Life Group leader and someone I have known since I was the age of sixteen stated that she did not remember me from the High School choir that I sang in for our church and where I had initially met her. It was very odd and very upsetting as we had already in other meetings discussed it. I believe the private investigation company had been working with a church Pastor to utilize these people and in her case put her up to this and was also recording our Life Group meetings. In one meeting she had an incident on her phone which played back my voice during our discussion. The other women also heard it and were a little upset as I was, and I then realized she had been recording us for a while as shortly after she asked if my email had been hacked. Since the Pastor was the only one, I told this to well once again God gave me my confirmation.

In mid-September I and another member spotted a person in a gray four door sedan waiting outside her house after our meeting. He drove away when he spotted us looking at him but then returned only to pass us and head down the street. We were in our cars by this time, so I followed him as I was concerned for her safety, but I believe not knowing I was following him he returned to her house. When he realized I had followed him he sped off going so fast I couldn't follow him so I called her from my car, and she said she would call her association president as there was a house down the way from her that had a history of drug interactions with the police involving their son and she thought maybe this car was waiting for someone. Not hearing back from her I contacted her, and she stated that the association president stated that this man in the car was probably just thinking she was "pretty" and that is why he was outside watching. Only one officer would say this, and he knows the Pastors, works at the church on some Sundays, attends the gym I attend and lives right next to the church. God once again confirmed that there was more surveillance occurring with no consideration that this Life group was to bring people together.

CHAPTER 22

THE GYMNASIUM

In November after the various encounters with the "church informers" the gym became a place identified where I could be found and as anybody knows this is not uncommon as most members go on certain days and quite often the same time. One day a man with a County Sheriff's shirt showed up at the gym; obviously wearing it prompting me to take notice helping him gain ground in striking up a conversation as he continued following me to various pieces of the equipment. This man was and still is a Sheriff at the County Jail working in the records department and I knew instantly someone had put him up to this especially with him wearing this type of shirt as it did draw attention to him and not just from me as others noticed him as well. He did finally come up to me smiling; actually, smirking is a better descriptive, and then proceeded to tell me many things about myself that he shouldn't have known. This was the first person that started stalking me at the gym and knowing someone put him up to this I outright asked him and continued to ask him, but he never admit this. He would stated he was interested in me but was married but wanted to have sex with me. It was at this point I did contact the front desk about his behavior but still wanting to confirm who put him up to this I continued inquiring but he would never say; he would just respond that "I was crazy," a typical "gas-lighting" method or tactic used quite often to get the victim to doubt themselves; I didn't. He then started talking to other people I knew in the gym which is, yet another tactic and a couple of people even came up to me and asked me how I knew him. I told them I didn't. I was not afraid of him because I knew he was a legitimate law enforcement officer, but I also knew he was assigned to entice me into being with him; possibly filming the encounter to use against me and this was not the last man to try this. He did eventually stop coming to the gym at least during the time I was there.

Another person who was a member of my church became the new person stalking me at the gym to gain information. I know the word stalking may seem inappropriate and I would agree as they did not come to my house, or business but it is still disconcerting to have people who you have never met come up to you at a gym as a plan to gain information. If anyone has ever attended a gym one knows it takes time to get to know people and even then, it is usually a conversation in passing; this has been at least my experience. I had never met her or had never seen her at the church. The first time I saw her she came up to me acting like she knew me much like the others. I did talk to her so that I could determine her motivation and she was from the church so I felt the need to at least hear her out. She brought up the church and the Pastor; trying to get me to speak ill of them which I did not, and she continued to try and be my friend over the next few months.

The monitoring did seem to increase at this point including their enlisting of various people showing up at the gym and I'm not sure they were paid for their services, but I am fairly sure that they utilized the FBI name, if in name alone, in their efforts. I believe some of these people at the gym did turn them down as I noticed a few people that were there during the week at the same time now were no longer attending at the same time. I also doubt that many of these informants ever asked their solicitors whether they had a court order to do this, and I also feel many were too afraid not to comply or depending on what they told them about me it may have made them feel important; this is probably truer than most people would admit.

My Friend the attorney

During this time, I did decide to confide in one of my friends who was part of my political group and an attorney. I believe someone contacted him as well but him being an attorney I believed he would only help law enforcement not one without authority. He invited a fellow attorney and a friend of his to meet as he was a civil rights attorney and was interested in hearing about the case. We all met once in my friend's office with them hearing the details of the hacking of my emails and sex offender issue but after this my friend kept canceling our appointments, so I decided to make an appointment to see his friend alone. This was not to keep him out of the conversation, but I did want to get it moving. When I arrived at his offices which was south of my location there was the local police presence once again and since I was a little early, I decided to drive down the street to get a coffee and once at this location as I was sitting in the parking lot there appeared two officers in their cars blatantly looking at me. I decided to head back to his office, and they did follow me but not into the parking lot. Upon my entering the building this attorney's assistant told me he had someone in his office but told me to take a seat. I don't believe he knew his assistant had informed me of this. When he came out of his office, he led me to another office close to the front of the building and proceeded to shut the door and drew the blinds. He then dialed someone on the phone which I assume was a speaker so that the person in his office could hear our conversation or even record it. I kept it brief due to the irregularities of this meeting and I am quite certain that the person in his office was my attorney friend listening in to the conversation and well quite possibly the local Police as well. When I did not send this attorney my written statement that I had promised him he sent a disclaimer to me registered mail that he would not take my case. The following day I viewed a local Police Sargent in his city showing up on my Facebook feed which seemed to be the start of at least confirming that law enforcement was always there when I was speaking to an attorney. It is possible that some attorney's that I had spoken with would not agree to record my conversation as it is illegal to do this in this state being a two-party consent state meaning all parties in the conversation have to agree to be recorded. This is one of the few good rules in this state and quite possibly some attorneys follow the law.

The Pandemic months

Due to what I called "The Manufactured Crisis" as early as March of 2020 much of my push to find out who was inhibiting me in my seeking justice slowed down considerably. Other odd occurrences however continued as I had run into a past acquaintance that I knew running into him twice in one week at a local store. I did ask him if he was stalking me and he just laughed and we met a couple of times in the parking lot sitting in our own cars speaking through the windows which many of my friends did this since most places were closed. He seemed determined to catch me in lies such as bringing up my being a little sister at Phi Kappa Sigma at a local University saying he didn't remember as he was there the same time I was there. It was obvious to me he was being employed by someone to get any kind of information on me. In September 2021 1 did meet at his insistence at a local restaurant as it was his birthday. He told me there would be other people attending that I knew but that turned out not to be true. We were dining out on the patio, and he kept asking me where my car was parked, I told him and at the end of the night he walked over to my car and hugged me which was very odd as I pushed him away, but I believe he had a picture taken just to confirm the meeting. He too has family that was on the police force but in the city.

There was also a man that I knew at the gym for a few years, no coincidence here for them to recruit from and he told me he was divorced and wanted to go out sometime. I gave him my number and I had his, but it was months before we were to go out as I wanted to be sure he was indeed divorced and I still had an uneasy feeling he was put up to this. He asked me out and we met at a local restaurant which he proceeded to bring up him getting arrested when he was young, him having cancer and the topic of surveillance so he obviously was being coached by someone but I believe he did have a conscience and most of these people do, it becomes hard for them to keep denying what they are doing and it is easier for them to avoid then admit what they have done. I haven't seen him since.

One of my friends, who I had known for thirty years originally meeting her at the local health club as she was the club's masseuse was now retired and she often invited me to join her on her patio which had a great view of a large pond and many friendly ducks; she loved her birds. One instance which was again suspicious was while on her patio we spotted a man sitting on a bench not far from us looking at his phone often but also viewing us from a distance. He did seem very out of place, and this continued the next time I visited her which was a week later and as I mentioned this to her she agreed and stated she had not seen him there any other time. The next day another friend of hers was visiting her and she mentioned this man to her as he walked by. Well, her friend being very outspoken asked him why he was there, and he proceeded to leave. She told me the next day she saw him out front and apologized for her friend's behavior and she said he stated that it was alright and not to worry but she never saw him there again. I do believe he was indeed monitoring our conversation and you must ask why else would he suddenly stop visiting except that he had been confronted?

In mid-June 2020 I sent an email to the Lead Pastor at my church requesting a meeting as I just wanted to clear the air and possibly stop the surveillance hoping they would confess they were part of it. He didn't respond to my email but the next morning there was a local police car sitting out front of my house and as soon as I left my house and as I drove by, he hid his face from me. The next day pulling out of my neighborhood I noticed him again but this time he turned in front of me making me come to a complete stop as he turned into the business next to my community. I let him pass and then proceeded to the next cross street stopping at the light and then turning left but within seconds I was pulled over by a different Police officer. I asked him why he had pulled me over and he did not respond but asked me for my license and went back to his vehicle for several minutes. When he approached me, he handed me my license back and asked what my address was. I had not updated my license due to the pandemic as the facilities were closed but did contact the state with my new address which is what I was instructed to do. I really believe this was prompted by the other officer to gain my address and he was going to let me go but at the last minute he stated he was going to give me a ticket stating that another officer in the store parking lot saw me on my phone. There was no other officer in that parking lot only the one that turned in front of me minutes earlier down the road. I explained to him that I was not on my phone but I was not going to argue with the police as police records can be accessed by other police departments, although not protocol they all work together. They will say this is not true but the officer I knew from the gym once said to me "you do know you have to pay cab drivers, right?" laughing right out loud after he said it and this tells me the cab incident which was deemed unlawful restraint and malicious prosecution and was supposed to be expunged was not and is still in the records that law enforcement can access.

CHAPTER 23

THE HACK

During the pandemic months my life group could not meet at our usual location, so it was at another member's house and at the very first meeting the topic of writing your story was brought up and I did confirm that I had done some writing and I believe she was looking to confirm this. She was also frequently asking me questions on why I was asked to step down from the security team. At one point I did believe that she should know the truth and not just what she heard in gossip and being tired of the innuendo I contemplated showing them something that would exonerate me. I do believe they did tell Pastor Miles of the book, and this was the start of a whole new wave of odd occurrences. I had been meeting with her and her husband occasionally as they were interested in our political group, but I was getting more hints that they were being utilized to find out information from me. Realizing this I thought I would show them something in writing so that they would possibly stop the questions and on October 20th I showed them an email concerning my FBI meeting that occurred in 2014. They said nothing, didn't have a follow up question and never brought it up to me again. I didn't hear from them until a few months later.

On November 12th I sent a message to this pastor that previously was at my church and who knew everything that had gone on in the last few years. I asked him why he would not answer my questions concerning what he knew about the investigation and surveillance of me and on November 13th my computer as I was logging in literally shut down denying me access. Not being able to log in I made an appointment with the local IT group at a store known for these services and confirmed I was indeed hacked and on November 17th I went into the store to pick up my laptop and upon review with a squad member much of my data was gone but my email was intact with a tag on it saying "Who does this?" I guess it referred to the many emails that were never deleted. I asked the young man if they wrote that and he said they did not and agreed with me it could be a message from the hacker. There was also a word document titled "Perfected for the Purpose" which was indeed my intellectual property; last updated in 2017. When I saw this, I asked him if he knew if the FBI or the local police were contacted but with this he stated "no it was the other way around." He wouldn't answer any more questions as he said he would get in trouble for telling me and not wanting to get this honest young man in trouble I left the store. I wanted to think about it knowing whoever hacked my system already had my book but now so did law enforcement. I wasn't concerned with them having it as I thought they would maybe uncover who did this and get in touch with me but sadly this did not happen. Them not moving on it even after filing a formal police report requesting an investigation is very telling in that most likely law enforcement knew who was responsible or knew someone with ties to them.

A few days later and while at the gym on November 20th I confirmed that the local police had my writings from none other than Mike Joseph, the same man who gave me Rich Steven's phone number in 2013 and one who kept inquiring about me and insinuating himself in my business for years. He started out by telling me that an author house had once offered him $350,000 to sell them his story. With this I knew and asked him outright if they had my book to which he stated yes and gave a little laugh. I believe they must have been monitoring my phone and heard this exchange or he informed them that I knew, and they then told him to stay away from me. From then on, he totally avoided me and since I only saw him at the gym this was not really a problem, but I do believe he not only told me of what they did but so did several other people. Now you have to ask who may have told him and since he has a son in law who is a policeman working in the area and he stated many times he was friends with a certain detective in the local department it didn't take much to determine who most likely informed him. It is my understanding that this detective's wife is also part of this police department. But there were others as well spreading the word from at least two officers that knew two previous neighbors of mine. This didn't seem to start until early 2021 however. These neighbors came up to me at the gym, again this is where I saw many people and well it became the place to seek me out as I had no other connection to them. They told me of another officer that confirmed that they had my writings. This seemed to cause many odd circumstances to transpire whether it was on Facebook or sent to me via email or odd texts.

On December 1, 2020 I noticed a detective from the city I lived in looking at my Facebook profile and after looking him up I did find out that he resided in the same town as a leader in my church. His address information changed shortly after uncovering this with it now reporting a new address and city for him but really any information can now be placed on the internet whether true or not. On December 4th I had a certain Pastor that I was not friends with also looking at my profile that originally knew of the sex offender and did nothing and on December 6th I had a man from a publishing company viewing my Facebook who also showed up at my gym for several weeks in February. On December 16th I had another officer looking at me on Facebook. During this time, I also continued to be stalked by that same woman from the church that started in 2019 but she now brought up that she had all her pictures from her computer stolen and she thought it was just a virus but I never even brought up being hacked or the book but of course somehow, she knew. She then told me her brother was a retired police officer and it does seem that with every informer that I encountered they had some connection to a law enforcement professional. This would make sense and actually a sure way to gain information without a warrant.

What came next was one of my credit cards being compromised and when I contacted the credit card company they requested information on a previous bank account which had absolutely nothing to do with this credit card. I do believe that I was not actually speaking to the company but I was speaking to some type of agency. I closed this account after this incident even though they stated they had no entry of this conversation. I also received a letter from a Fertility company that stated it was an IT platform for many infertility clinics including Fertility Centers in my state and that on September 14, 2020 they experienced a security event that may have compromised my privacy concerning my health information. They then proceeded to state that on December 4, 2020 that my information was accessed including my social security number and patient number/MPI. They stated they believed there was no misuse of my information but that I should contact them to freeze my account and that I would have to supply them my private information. This was such a confirmation in so many ways as I never was involved in any fertility clinic however my writings discussed my ovarian failure and I believe through this tactic they thought they could gain access to my medical records.

CHAPTER 24

PRESENT DAY

The harassment unfortunately continues, and it is now 2023 and my case still to this day is not resolved. As far as employment, most any position I applied for; even being overqualified resulted in a denial after running a background check and this even after eleven years of when it happened and of my case being expunged; records never go away. I did become fortunate that a wonderful family-owned company did offer me a job but right before I started someone contacted my superior telling them of my record; followed by his law enforcement family member looking me up to confirm. This is illegal and this is one more reason that police reform does need to be taken seriously. In any case I am still working but the information on my writings were not only investigated once again but were shared with the police department responsible for this injustice against me. This most likely made the handful of men responsible very angry wanting to retaliate and insure they are never held responsible for their actions in 2012.

The police report I made on the infiltration of my computer in 2020 was never investigated per their response, at least not for my benefit and based on a my more recent FOIA request it was deemed not investigated, administratively closed and that all public access was and is denied. They have covered themselves in every area but it is obvious the story is still out there as the States Attorney's office continues their game of making deals and collecting fabulous fees and punishing me for speaking to the FBI.

I hope this does change with the publishing of this and maybe more people will stand up and come forward and do the right thing and expose the illegal activity as it does in the end come down to the courts.

**He who began a good work in you will carry
it on to completion until the day of Christ Jesus
Philippians 1:6**

FURTHER PROOF

Confirmation of The Corruption

We are all aware of the corruption in our court system, but it continues because it works for many, the attorneys', the prosecutors, the judges and the guilty who can pay their way out of their troubles. There are so many stories of corruption, and I am sure many can relay their own stories or they have heard stories from family or friends so these may not surprise you but what is important is when your reading the following please remember these stories all came to me and I did not seek them out. God is close to me, and I listen to him and in this case, I believe he supplied me with this additional proof if only to share with those that may not be aware.

Case #1

In the spring of 2013 at the same time, I was going through the early phase of my ordeal and while watching the Sunday morning news the mug shot of the son of an acquaintance of mine appeared on the screen. He had been arrested and charged with murder in a gang related incident; the deceased being an innocent bystander just walking his dog that night. Since Shaun was driving the car he was also charged with murder as was his friend, holding codefendants responsible. Shaun, who is white and from a wealthy family was acquitted by our very same Judge Frank Thomas and according to Shaun's mother it cost them two college educations to buy their way out of it. His friend who was said to have shot the gun; Hispanic and poor received forty years behind bars. I was told by his mother that it cost them dearly to get their son off and I guess you can't blame them for loving their son but what about this poor soul who at the age of 23 was sentenced to 45 years behind bars or in reality, most of his life. What were the chances this would happen right in my own backyard where this type of violence was rare but that I would also know him and his family? But a bright light appeared and again, God gave me the opportunity to learn more about the system as I ran into Shaun's mother in 2018 and she told me the case was overturned and the young man was now free. Interestingly enough the prosecutor and Judge, that being Frank Thomas were both cited for misconduct on their part. I did confirm this information on the internet that same day but the next day the information was nowhere to be found as anything can be taken down paying the various services; luckily, I documented this before they took it down. One does have to wonder how they knew I looked it up but that is of course possible as well. I hear that the young man of course sued and won his case but only against the law enforcement that were involved in his case and there is no information about the judges or prosecutor's accountability for their roles. This is not uncommon as anything can disappear from public access and we the taxpayers paid for their corruption.

Case # 2

Another case in point a few years later and a further example of the corruption concerned a young man who had several; nine to be exact, driving citations including driving at high speeds, reckless driving and driving while intoxicated. This young man through his actions and the corruption of our court system allowed him to never be charged resulting in him finally killing someone, specifically a mother, a father and their daughter. The court system failed them all as he also lost his life. His attorney who got him off all of these previous violations was not available for comment, and this is not surprising. His name is part of public records, but they pay to keep their names off the internet at all costs. It is very sad that people continue to look the other way and concede that's just how things are done. The remaining daughter surely settled for some huge amount through suggestion of council, suing the parents of this man and she also sued the state for negligence and us the taxpayers payed once again. This young man's record was obtained by one of the last honest investigative journalists in this state otherwise it wouldn't have made the news. Thank you for these warriors with a conscience, we need to listen to them and filter the rhetoric. They stated in the news report that the young man never lost his license because of an existing point system utilized in our state; yet again the deception continues. I only hope the Bureau's White-Collar Crime Division will step in and investigate the practices in the court system in this state and specifically this county. They have had many opportunities and continue to look the other way, possibly they feel it's just not that important.

Case # 3

So, there are those that are caught and want it to go away and will throw all sorts of money at it and well there are those that are chronic abusers quite often alcoholics that are caught driving while drinking time and time again only to buy their way out of their troubles. A case in point comes to mind and happened a few years ago and while out with a friend watching a game at a local restaurant, I met a man who worked at a dealership and being in the market for a new car we exchanged cards. Well, nothing prepared me for this but he called me the next day and left a message that he enjoyed meeting me even though he got into a little trouble that night. I text him that it was nice meeting him and asked him what he meant of which he never responded but I did receive a call from a friend of his later that day that I had never met telling me that he was arrested, being held in the County jail and had three prior DUI's and if I didn't help him he was going to jail. Wow wrong person to divulge this information to and I told her I couldn't help him. I then got a call from the Public Defender's office asking me to testify on his behalf. I proceeded to tell her I didn't know him and certainly could not testify to how much he had been drinking as I had just met him for a few minutes and she told me she understood. Now you have to ask why this would happen to me unless God wanted to once again show me and give me proof on how prevalent this corruption is in our court system. When you are acquitted the process continues and of course if you have money you will further fund the court system and an attorney in preparing your expungement. You know maybe if he was held responsible he wouldn't be where he is today which most assuredly is jail but on the flip side had he gotten off once again, he could have killed someone having one more opportunity to drink and drive.

Case #4

I continued to have more encounters that only confirmed to me that my sharing of what I went through was indeed to be shared with others. I call these divine encounters from God, giving me more ammunition confirming the need for uncovering the truth about the justice system and those that take advantage of it. The next example involved a co-worker that had heard of my marketing background and asked me if I wanted to make some money working on a marketing plan for him. I asked him to explain further and he proceeded to tell me of a company in another state that allowed you to pay your way out of tickets through their website assigning a lawyer to your case and insuring a not guilty verdict or your money back. He told me he had thirteen attorneys on board representing the various counties in this state. He would make fifty dollars off the top for each referral but also shielding the attorneys from illegal solicitation. I asked him who the attorneys were and he supplied me with three of their names.

Again, you have to ask was this by chance that this type of illegal activity was presented to me and so very clearly detailed? Nothing is by chance. I said I would think about it and proceeded to once again do the right thing and escalate it to my contact requesting his thoughts on the matter with him telling me to not do this on my own and strongly urged me to not get involved. A few days later I was confronted by my co-worker that he no longer was interested in this venture but prompted me to call these attorney's and speak to them about doing the business myself, which I did not. He also informed me he was pulled over not once but twice that weekend by police so I do believe this information I gave to Cameron Peters was passed on or was possibly heard by surveillance which is entirely possible, I don't know. This man seemed so pleasant and polite I was curious why he was involved in this type of business so I decided to ask him. He told me he was divorced and had two young children and when I asked how he knew so many attorneys' he told me that some he had hired and the rest were referrals. He had been in trouble with the law since he was in his early teens and he told me me he spent time in jail, learning the system and how it works. He thought nothing of paying his way out of trouble and told me that he didn't create the system it was just the way it was and he couldn't be responsible and why not get some of the reward. I then proceeded to avoid him while also wondering what kind of man he may have been if he had been held responsible for his actions in his youth. We do not do our children any favors by demonstrating they can buy their way out of their troubles while applauding the attorney for their illegal behavior.

Case #5

One other story that was in the news is about a man who was hit by a passing car while he was in a crosswalk. This man has suffered terribly; medically and financially and the man who ran him down not only tried to elude police but also had four priors and currently had no license. This man received a one-year probation sentence.

The states attorney commented when questioned that it was his first offense but please tell that to the man that you almost killed and his family who has had to endure this hardship. I am fairly certain someone paid his way out of it or as is the case in this county the states attorney is being more lenient with some nationalities over others and is not following the rule of law in sentencing and this relatively new behavior is most likely in retaliation to the many years that certain nationalities were unjustly accused and convicted based on their race. In this case this man had the money and for those that have the money and can afford a favorable verdict it often comes down to what the market will bear.

Case #6

Yet another case came to my attention from an elderly woman I had met in political group we both attended. She wanted to tell me her story and I don't even know how this topic came up but it was clear I needed to hear her. It seems she was sideswiped by a passing car going too fast causing a substantial amount of damage to the right side of her car. The driver did not stop, so she called 911 and followed him until the police pulled him over. He was clearly guilty as the police on sight confirmed and ticketed him but during the court appearance which she was present for the Judge in the case asked the transcriber to stop and leave the court room while he heard this man's testimony and then proceeded to find him not guilty. I confirmed this man was very wealthy and well one can surmise how this victorious verdict came about. And again, I did not seek her story out, she shared it with me.

Case #7

I was having lunch with a friend that I knew from church and I also knew her family and as well, her daughter. We were just finishing up when her daughter and new boyfriend showed up to talk to us which seemed very odd to me but I believe everything happens for a reason and this was not any different to the many stories. It wasn't five minutes into the conversation that her daughter blurted out that she had been arrested months earlier for driving while under the influence and also possession of a controlled substance. I do believe they had planned for her to stop by, bring this up to find out more about what happened to me. The gossip in this church is widespread and I thought she was a friend but friends do not deceive their friends but it did confirm that someone had informed her within the church. I did not tell her of my experience but decided to hear her daughter out and as she was relaying her experience the story was so very similar to what I experienced I at first questioned whether it even happened but I did confirm later she was indeed arrested. She stated the arresting officer continued to flirt with her the entire time as he searched her car with no probable cause and of course warrant and then took her to the hospital for a blood test to determine whether she had taken the drug and of course her intoxication level. She was then taken to the local jail where she remained until the next morning to appear in court and she then was taken to the county jail where she was held for another ten hours, her story mirroring my story so I am sure this happens often, especially to women. She stated that the drug charge was dismissed even though she did indeed have a small bag of cocaine in the backseat of her car but with the officer never showing up in court the case was thrown out. Again, not following the law and obviously a payout from her attorney.

Closing

In closing we at this moment in time have a new law passed by congress that has gone to the Supreme court in this state; ruling on its constitutionality. I believe in the rule of law and the safety it provides but one does have to acknowledge that the many past incidences of corruption in our law enforcement and in our courts has prompted this new bill. I know God has made this happen if only to serve those that have experienced this type of injustice and possibly then the scale will truly be balanced.

Printed in the United States
by Baker & Taylor Publisher Services